BY JESS JOHNSTON

I'll Be There (But I'll Be Wearing Sweatpants)
(with Amy Weatherly)

Here for It (the Good, the Bad, and the Queso)
(with Amy Weatherly)

Perfect
Is Boring
(And It Tastes
Like Kale)

Perfect Is Boring (And It Tastes Like Kale)

FINDING BELONGING AND PURPOSE

WITHOUT CHANGING WHO YOU ARE

Jess Johnston

CONVERGENT

NEW YORK

Published in the United States by Convergent Books, an imprint of Random House, a division of Penguin Random House LLC, New York.

CONVERGENT with colophon is a registered trademark of Penguin Random House LLC.

LIBRARY OF CONGRESS CATALOGING-IN-PUBLICATION DATA
Names: Johnston, Jess, 1985– author.
Title: Perfect is boring (and it tastes like kale) / by Jess Johnston.
Description: First edition. | New York, NY: Convergent, [2025] |
Identifiers: LCCN 2024019972 (print) | LCCN 2024019973 (ebook) |
ISBN 9780593728246 (hardcover; alk. paper) |
ISBN 9780593728253 (ebook)
Subjects: LCSH: Self-acceptance. | Self-perception. | Self-realization. |
Perfectionism (Personality trait)
Classification: LCC BF575.S37 J65 2025 (print) | LCC BF575.S37 (ebook) |
DDC 158.1—dc23/eng/20240703
LC record available at https://lccn.loc.gov/2024019972
LC ebook record available at https://lccn.loc.gov/2024019973

Printed in Canada on acid-free paper

convergentbooks.com

2 4 6 8 9 7 5 3 1

First Edition

Book design by Caroline Cunningham
Frontispiece: AdobeStock/dariaustiugova

To Graham:
This book would never have been written if it weren't for your sacrifice and passionate support of my dreams. Thank you for championing me so selflessly and for loving us all so well. Thank you for your perfectly timed comedic relief and for never taking me too seriously. Thank you for being my home. I love you.

To Malachi:
I am so proud of you and so proud of the way you run after your dreams. Keep having fun, turning up the music so I can hear your car coming from a mile away (literally), and going after life with your whole heart. Stay confidently in your lane; it will take you there.

To Scout:
I love you, my cave son. I love that you never remember to bring your shoes anywhere and are a passionate connoisseur of the tuna melt. Keep being you because you're fantastic (and hilarious).

To Oaklee:
I love your creative and gentle nature, and I also love your fierceness and your fire. Don't doubt yourself for a second; you are magic.

To Haven:
I love your wild. Keep taking up lots of space. Your voice and your passion inspire me. You are a beautiful, sparkling, colorful whirlwind, and I'm here for it.

To Mom and Dad (Chuck and Susan):
Thank you for being such beautiful inspirations to all of us.

To Josh:
The only one who was there for all of it and inspires me to this day with his ingenuity and good heart. I love you, brother.

To Benji and Aubree,
who have become family. Thank you for being our adventure buddies.

CONTENTS

-- -- ---- -- ------ -- ------- -- --

PART ONE

--- ---- ---- ---- ---- ---- ----- ---- ---- ----

PART TWO

- - - - - - -

PART THREE

- - - - - - -

INTRODUCTION

Confessions of a Big, Gigantic Failure (Who Learned to Love Herself as She Is)

I don't know about you, but being perfect never worked for me. Some people are probably cut out for it. Martha Stewart, maybe? Daniel Tiger's mom? The queen? But not me. I'm naturally messy, naturally undetailed, naturally scattered, naturally feely.

I was aiming to be the MVP of my household for a while. I was going to be so organized, so on top of it, so good at using the cute planner that I'd purchased. Then my garbage cans got repossessed. I didn't know that was a thing, but it is. I forgot to pay that bill, and one morning I woke up and they'd taken them back. The county was like, *Take that! Welcome to consequences, you no longer deserve a city trash can.*

I tried hard, but my flaws kept showing up anyway, like a stain on the carpet that keeps coming back every time it dries. Turns out I'm better at just being me, a woman in her late thirties who has lost about nine hundred debit cards, gets grumpy with her kids and husband sometimes, hyperventilates when she laughs hard, loves ranch dressing, and only shaves her ankles in the wintertime. I'm a mess, but I'm me, and I like myself better this way (I can say that now). It was like I'd been wearing jeans that dug in and also made me feel angry. Then I realized I could buy new jeans—or better yet, leggings.

The truth is, I don't think I ever really wanted to be perfect, not really. I wanted to belong, and I was convinced to my core that the reason I was lonely was that I wasn't doing "it" right. I wasn't talking right, living right, eating and exercising right, and if I just did better, I wouldn't hurt so much.

Can you relate?

I've been writing for hundreds of thousands of women (plus about ten dads, five grandpas, and the occasional internet creeper) for nearly a decade now, and this is what I've discovered:

We are really, really hard on ourselves.

We imagine there is a standard we must live up to. Said standard is also certifiably impossible. We also sort of know this, and it doesn't help.

We believe that if we just "did better," "worked harder," "were less messy/flawed/human," our life would be infinitely better, and we (and everyone else) would like us more, therefore giving us the belonging we want so desperately.

We compare way the heck too much, and social media has not helped us in that area.

We have things that we think are wrong with us specifically, and us only (or maybe like one or two other losers). We basically think we are one in a million, but in a bad way. We think this about big things (*no one I know struggles to be patient with my kids like I do*) and small things (*no one's fridge crisper looks as disgusting as my fridge crisper*).

According to my research, there are a few things that make us feel better:

Learning that someone else's crisper has rotten vegetables in it. (Bonus points if you assumed this person was more together than you.)

Learning that every single one of us has some version of the crisper. Maybe it isn't buying-then-avoiding-produce specifically, but it's something.

You guys, good news:

First, I currently (like right now) have a rotting bag of sliced bell peppers in my crisper. I imagined I was going to make fajitas. I was a different person then, full of dreams and possibilities. I did not make fajitas (I would have, but I forgot I ever wanted to do that), and now here we are. The peppers are soft enough to make me gag and never cook them, but they're not moldy enough for me to throw away without guilt. Naturally, I'll need to let them become three times as disgusting before I can part with them.

Second, *it's true.* We all (every single last one of us) have our version of the crisper.

What's your crisper? What's your version of "I struggle to be patient with my kids"?

Do you have a hard time making friends? You're introverted and you'd rather keep to yourself, so you do.

Do you wrestle with anxiety or depression?

Do you put yourself on the back burner (like the farthest back, nearly out of reach)? You want to prioritize yourself, but you don't even know where to begin.

Do you have shame around your marriage because it just hasn't turned out the way you expected and you're not sure how to fix it?

Do you have something you're battling silently? Something you're scared to talk about because you're pretty sure no one would understand?

We don't need to share our deepest secrets and fears with everyone, but we can intentionally look for other women who are safe and ready to handle them. We can present a more real, more authentic version of ourselves to the world.

I've learned that when we share our less-than-put-together selves with other women, we offer them keys to freedom—and we step into freedom ourselves. There is power in our corporate messiness, more power than we ever could have imagined.

The answers we're looking for aren't in the crisper, and they're not in the next fad diet we're considering, either. The answers lie in leaning into our flaws and our gifts. They're in inviting belonging through our own risk and vulnerability; in living with purpose in our own way. Not our neighbor's way, not our friend's way, not our celebrity idol's way, and not even fit-debbie-45 on Instagram's way. (I made that up; sorry if there is really a fit-debbie-45.)

The answers are in us already. They're in wearing shoes that fit, in letting ourselves be ourselves, and in accepting that we're a lot—a lotta mess, and a lotta great, too.

My in-laws owned an old farmhouse just off the highway in Creston, Montana, for over thirty years. My mother-in-law, Marie, made it beautiful all year round. She planted a Canadian maple that turned bright red in the fall, lilacs that bloomed in the spring, and flowers that exploded out of boxes and beds whenever the soil was thawed enough to plant in. The summertime brought nightly dinners at a long picnic table with linen tablecloths and pitchers of sweet tea.

It was a landmark to everyone who drove by. A tire swing hung from one of the tallest branches of massive cottonwoods in the front yard, and vines clung to the lattice by the kitchen windows. In the winter every ridge of the roof was lined with twinkle lights. When you walked up the front steps, you could smell Marie's fresh-baked chocolate mayonnaise cake. Candles were always lit, and carefully chosen antiques and textiles pulled you in with their warmth.

It was beautiful but not curated. There were half-finished projects in front of the shed and tools that got forgotten on the porch step. There was a pile of papers on the hutch and socks and laundry on the bottom of the stairs, which the kids always forgot to take up. It wasn't perfect, but that made it better. It was a scene you could place yourself in, not like that house you visited as a kid that was beautiful in a magazine way, but your mom whisper-commanded in your ear to please not touch anything and for the love, use your napkin at dinner.

It was home. Not just my in-laws' home, but home to every person who walked through the doors. It was the kind of home you could laugh in, be rowdy in, and make mistakes in.

In the center of their kitchen was a long red table. It was worn with scratches, scuffs, and warped edges that paid homage to thousands of shared meals and lively conversations. Anyone who ever walked through those doors remembers that table. They might not remember what they ate or what they talked about (unless it was that mayonnaise cake, because it's life changing), but they remember how they felt. They felt welcomed. They felt like they belonged. The proof covered their refrigerator: family pictures and cards held by clunky magnets from people all over the world who had once shared a meal there. They all said the same thing: *Thank you for treating us like family*, and *We want our house to be just like your house.*

My first time in their kitchen, I was eighteen years old, and Graham and I were still hanging out "as friends." There were always extras at their house: someone who needed a place to stay for a while, friends who had become family, someone from church who just happened to drop by at dinnertime. Place settings were pushed closer and closer together, and extra chairs were brought from the basement. Someone wheeled in an office chair, and I squeezed onto a bench between Graham and one of his sisters, trying not to bump anyone with my elbows. The room was alive and vibrant as everyone shared stories, laughed, and shouted to please pass the bread. Marie glowed with joy and laughed louder than anyone as she put hot trays on the table. Someone spilled their drink and no one cared except to laugh while the party continued and a rag was tossed across the table. The drink was refilled without so much as a pause.

It was a home and a table to do life at.

Don't tell, but I might have fallen in love with Graham's family and that table before I fell in love with him. I was walking out of the loneliest years of my life, a season when I had sacrificed everything, even my health and well-being, for the sake of being what I thought was "perfect." I was recently (and precariously) in my first year of recovery from an eating disorder, unsure if where I was headed was safer than where I came from. I dabbled in old habits, still convinced that was what it took to be wanted, to be chosen, to belong. It was the happiest surprise to find out that belonging actually happened in a farmhouse kitchen with homemade bread and thick chunks of butter. It was found in eating and sharing, laughing and talking. It meant showing up wholeheartedly with quirks and flaws and messes to find I had a seat at the table. I would discover later that it was found in creating belonging, not seeking it.

Eating at that table invited me to a different kind of life, and I was all in, immediately. It was salvation for my very exhausted heart.

In life, I think there are two kinds of tables. There is the kind made for tiptoeing around other people's imagined opinions, full-face makeup, slapping a smile over our pain, and faking our way to a perceived acceptance. At that table, we're told that we need to fall in line, follow the rules, hide our weaknesses, lead with our achievements, be fine when we're not fine, and act impressive to gain acceptance. No matter how well we perform, no matter how successful we are at playing the part, no matter what important people we're seated next to, it will feel empty.

I don't know about you, but I got tired of feeling like I was walking through a cluttered antiques store with a backpack on. (I'm picturing Kim's Antiques from *Gilmore Girls*. If you know, you know.) It's not a question of if I break something, it's when.

What if we flipped the script and this wasn't actually a thing? What if life was for trying stuff out, breaking out in random dance, and making mistakes? I'd much rather life be more like a trampoline park, where tripping and falling just adds to the fun.

Perfect is boring. Let's not do that anymore. I know I don't want to.

This book is for every girl who has ever scribbled in her diary, *I don't know what's wrong with me*. It's for every mom who has ever thrown up her hands in despair, saying, "I try so hard, and I can't seem to get it right." It's for anyone who's felt like an outsider, unsure how she'd ever get in. It's for every girl who's ever gone on a crash diet trying to be a size she had no business being. It's for every woman who has ever gone through a breakup and thought it was because she was too _____. It's for every girl who has ever snapped at her family and melted into a puddle of shame thinking, *Why can't I just get it together?* It's also for a special, slightly more specialized group (spoiler, me): the kind who manages to lose their keys like twenty times a week. It's for all of us. It might not be the crisper; it could be an anxiety diagnosis. Whatever it is, we're in it together.

This book is an invite to my table, the one Graham and I have built together. (It isn't red, but it has spots of pen and paint from the kids' art projects.) This table is meant for sweatpants and bare feet, good days and bad days, days when your makeup is on point and those when you're rocking your dark under-eye circles. This table is made for real and it's made for honesty. When you're sitting here, you don't feel tired from pretending, you feel refreshed from being known. It's not perfect or curated, but it's real, authentic, and warm (and I make killer tacos). I hope it feels the way walking into Marie's kitchen for the first time felt for me.

This book is both an invitation and the tools you need to invite belonging and live with purpose—but as you are already, not as someone you must strive to become.

In each chapter, I will address one of the myths that keep us stuck in our own heads, drowning in perfectionism, filled with I'm-not-enough energy, and trying to fit in at tables we were never meant to sit at. Myths like: "If I'm rejected, I will die" (you will not, I promise), "It's better not to try than to try and fail" (how's that working for you? Great for me, too), and "I'm a junior varsity adult" (talking and drinking Gatorade is nice, but it's time to get off the bench and *play*). Let's throw out the whole mess and start over.

Let me tell you a story (a lot of stories actually) of how I went from a girl who hated her flaws and was at war with her body to one who thinks her flaws are some of the greatest things about her.

Ya ready?

Imagine I'm swinging open the door to my house. The music is too loud from my recent rage cleaning (yes, that's 2Pac and Dr. Dre), and I still have a broom in my hand, which I throw to the side so I can welcome you in. I happily talk to you over the music like you can hear me (you cannot). You shout "WHAT?" and I realize my mistake, jog over to my speaker, and turn it down. I puff up one throw pillow. (I'm weird about my throw pillows, okay? The house could be burning down around us, but the pillows need to be right.) I quickly close a door and explain that I don't really have a junk drawer right now, it's more like a junk room, but the good news is if you need a snorkel or a hoodie for any reason, I've probably got one in there. I tell you that I'm making french fries (I don't know, it just feels right). I pour us each a drink and we sit down at the table.

Hey friend, I'm so glad you're here. Let's sit and talk for a while. How are you, and I mean really? (Please give me the long version with all the TMI, I'm here for it.)

P.S. I don't even hate kale that much. I just like things that taste good better.

PART ONE

Lies That Keep Us from Loving Ourselves as We Are

(Or, Becoming an Imperfectionist)

LIE #1: Today I'll Be Perfect

10/06/2019

Dear Diary,

I couldn't find my keys again.

After looking for an eternity (okay, ten minutes . . .), I was about to give up and resign myself to a life of biking forever. It's fine, I can pick up all four kids from school on my handlebars. Graham asked me if I threw them away, which was offensive.

They were in the trash.

Love,

Jess

The high school doors loomed ominously in front of me, and I felt sick. I glanced behind me. Should I make a run for it? But a river of students flooded into the entrance, pulling me with them. Laughter, shouting, and the clanging of lockers opening and shutting merged into an indecipherable cloud of noise.

I was the new kid again, and I wanted to be anywhere in the whole world but here. A group of gorgeous girls walked past me, their Abercrombie jeans hugging just below their hips, their long straight hair flowing behind them, and their perfume wafting over me like a secret they would never tell. I was suddenly hyperaware of my clothes and the way my hair frizzed instead of lying flat. I shifted the weight of my backpack on my bony shoulder, my T-shirt and pants still hanging off me, even though I was six months into recovery from a yearlong battle with anorexia. The bell rang and my soul left my body, the school spreading out in front of me like a maze. I couldn't be late. It would just be one more thing to add to my list of screwups and things that were wrong with me.

JESSICA CUSHMAN:

Tall, but surprisingly bad at basketball (she blames her small feet). Five foot nine and size seven and a half shoe, in case you were wondering.

Tries to blend in, but kinda sticks out in a bad way, like you might trip over her (again, very tall).

Bad sense of direction and zero navigation skills (that's why she is definitely going to be late to first period).

Face turns bright red after any and all physical exertion. You might think she needs a hospital, she does not, it's just her face.

Organization style is "shove papers in bag, in drawer, in locker, and never throw anything away just in case." Definitely doesn't know where her class schedule is or where that sticky note with her locker combination went.

Person she identifies with the most from 1990s rom-coms: Josie Geller from *Never Been Kissed*.

The whole day felt like one of those dreams where you've lost your voice. The only thing more terrifying than class was the snack breaks between periods, when other kids congregated and I took laps up and down the hall as if I had somewhere to go so I wouldn't seem like the friendless loser that I was. At lunchtime I hid in a bathroom stall, tucked my feet up on the toilet lid in case they checked beneath the stalls, and cried. The only outlet for my pain was tossing the sandwich from home in the garbage. I couldn't control a single thing in my life except that sandwich. I just knew that the world wouldn't hurt so badly if I were more. More what? Um, everything.

Have you felt it? Do you know what I mean? I just wish I could hug you in the moment when you first experienced this, and I wish I could hug me, too. We were never meant to feel this way.

Our stories are all different, but over the last decade of writing, I've talked to hundreds of thousands of women who struggle to accept themselves as they are. They struggle with feeling that they lack something, that they're not quite enough, and that somehow (at the exact same time) they are far too much.

It's hard to be a woman.

If we're organized and driven, we feel bad that we're not more easygoing and spontaneous. We wrestle with shame because we're human in our parenting, friendships, and marriages, not superheroes who never make mistakes. We question our value because we don't look like fitness models—and if we are fitness models, we still question our value and have deep insecurities over our hair or skin. Speaking of hair, we wish we brushed it more and remembered to clean the receipts out of the side-door compartment of our car, or we wish we weren't so uptight about keeping everything organized just right. We wish we slowed down more to enjoy the moment, or we wish we were more driven and had more purpose in our lives (sometimes we wish both at the same time, and that's confusing). At a surface level, our hair is too flat, too curly, too stringy; our hips are too wide, too womanly, too narrow, too boyish. On a deeper level, we are too sensitive, too passive, too intense, too angry, too bossy.

We apologize constantly, for being human, or for being incapable of being seventeen places at once. We feel guilty for missing bake sales and volunteer hours because we're working full-time, or not joining that family vacation because we can't afford it. There is no winning. There is only trying and trying until we're sick, tired, and disillusioned.

About a decade ago, I made a friend named Aubree (you're going to hear a lot about her). Aubree changed my life. From day one, she was frighteningly real. "How's it going?" I'd ask her if I ran into her in town. "It's pretty horrible today, actually," she'd say. "I'm struggling with some things and just not feeling great."

Her authenticity terrified me, but it also intrigued me. I was busy channeling my best Pollyanna. *I'm happy! Maybe the happiest! Marriage is great, thanks for asking. Motherhood is great, too. I love not sleeping, smelling like sour milk, and losing every shred of my identity. It's my favorite.*

When I was around Aubree, I felt at ease in my own skin, and I began opening up about my struggles. It was a learning process, though. She'd ask how I was doing (in a way that was sincere, like she really wanted to know), and I'd feel like I'd just been delivered a pop quiz from my high school chemistry teacher. *Good? Is that the right answer? I mean maybe I'm not good. I haven't cried in years, and I feel disconnected from my heart. This is hard. How much of my grade does this count for, because if it's not a lot, can we go to the next question?*

One morning, Aubree texted me when I was in the middle of household chaos. So far, I'd broken up five different sibling rivalries, fished a Tonka truck out of the toilet, and begged my kids to just eat their breakfast (and then cleaned most of said breakfast out of the rug). *Hey want to meet at the beach?* she asked. I started to text *Sounds great!* and stopped myself. Instead, I wrote: *Hi, everything is a crapshoot today. I'm tired and grumpy and my kids are crazy. I can come, but I'm probably not going to be much fun.*

Her response changed my life: *I don't care if you're fun or not fun. I like you both ways.*

It was one text out of the thousands we've now sent, but I've never forgotten it. Aubree's graciousness and acceptance of me (in all my sweaty, dirty-messy-bun, under-caffeinated, uptight glory) caused shame I didn't even realize I was feeling to almost physically lift off me. The stress of that particular morning was just a sampling of the pressure I felt most days. It wasn't simply about the Tonka truck or the rug; it was deeper than that. It was the invisible mental load that really weighed me down: the weight of expectation I felt as a woman.

There's a post I see sometimes on Instagram: "I don't know who needs to hear this, but unclench your jaw." (It's me. I'm the one who needs to hear it.) If you just thought, *It's me, too, I was totally clenching,* let's take a second.

Unclench your jaw.

Soften your forehead.

Drop your shoulders.

Roll your head gently to the right and to the left.

Wiggle your toes.

Breathe deep.

You're not alone.

According to a recent poll, 71 percent of millennial women said it's their job to be the chief worry officer (CWO) in their household (I felt that). Eighty-two percent felt that although it's well known that women are overburdened, no one is doing anything about it. For that reason, 74 percent are worried about the mental state of their friends. The study also asked them to describe their current mental state. The top words used were *stressed, anxious, tired, depressed,* and *confused.* I don't care if you're millennial, Xennial, or Generation X, it affects us all.

What words would you use to describe your current mental

state? I'd like to add *frazzled* to the mix, or maybe *juggling feral cats.* It's not until someone like Aubree gives us permission to be human that we realize how heavy our load is and how tired we are.

What are you stressed about today? Maybe this morning you had a fight with your teenager and you feel terrible. Maybe you just checked your bank account and realized it's been a full year that you've been paying for that gym membership (and not going). Maybe you put your foot in your mouth really badly the other day and you can't stop thinking about it. Maybe your list of to-dos is longer than your actual life span. Maybe you're just bone-tired and you don't know why.

There's a lot "wrong" with me. I've got anxiety, I have ADHD, I'm incredibly scatterbrained, and I cook only on high heat (because simmering is far too tedious and slow). I'm impatient, I'm inconsistent, I'm horrible at keeping track of my checking account, and once I got two parking tickets for the exact same spot two days in a row (which my husband finds mind-blowing). I'm sensitive and a little moody, happy and disorganized. If you leave a Pyrex at my house, there's a 100 percent chance I'll just think that I forgot I owned two Pyrexes. The good news is, you can feel free to dig through my cupboards and take what is yours. Heck, take something of mine, I won't notice that, either.

I don't care how old I get or how healthy I am, there are still rooms I walk into that bring me right back to that acute feeling of *I don't belong here,* followed by a wave of shame as I complete the sentence: "I don't belong here because I am not _____ enough." The feeling is so real, so potent, that it takes my breath away.

Do you know the feeling?

It's the feeling of there being an invisible set of rules for belonging, and everyone got a list but you.

It's the feeling of walking into a meeting convinced that everyone is more qualified than you and you're an imposter.

It's the feeling of meeting someone new and not being able to think of a single thing to say and then the awkwardness hangs in the air and you finally break the silence with something like, "I have heartburn because I can't stop eating cheese late at night." Then they just kind of smile and don't respond, and you're like, *OMG, I'm never speaking again.*

It's the feeling from that dream where you're in a crowd and suddenly realize you're not wearing pants.

In my years of writing and researching women and friendship, here's what I've found: Perfectionism and performance might help us "fit in" to societal standards, but they will never help us belong.

In fact, perfectionism and performance are two of the main reasons we feel lonely. "Having it all together" won't make us feel like we belong, but acknowledging (to the right people) that we don't have it all together will. If there's one thing we universally have in common, it's flaws. Anyone who tells you otherwise is lying.

Connection is found in our real, not our perfect. We're not going to feel belonging if we don't show up as who we are. We will stay lonely, even if we have a thousand friends. Period.

The U.S. surgeon general has declared loneliness an epidemic, affecting more people in our country than diabetes. It's sucking the life out of us, literally. I read a line in *USA Today* recently that jumped off the page at me: "If you're feeling lonely, you're not alone."

It's not just that we're lonely, it's that we believe we are alone in our loneliness. It's another perceived flaw to add to the list, because at our core we believe we're alone in our humanity and brokenness. That's why I think social media has made the problem worse, not better. We can put on a cute outfit and get the very best angle, or post a picture of our living room from the five minutes it wasn't covered in crumbs and toddler toys. It might give us the false feeling of pride momentarily, but it isn't sustained because it's not real. Connection that is rooted in performance will never make us feel less lonely. What we're craving is people who will walk in our living room when there's laundry to be folded and sippy cups on the floor and sit with us right smack dab in the middle of it and say, "I see you and you're all right."

Whether you're sixteen years old and hiding in a bathroom stall, or forty-six and questioning your ability to parent a sixteen-year-old (and not lose it over all the mugs growing a fungus somewhere in their room), this is for you. Belonging and purpose aren't found in striving; they're found in accepting and sharing.

They're found in texting a friend just exactly how you are doing and then showing up to the beach with a quad espresso and a T-shirt with a stain on it. They're found sitting cross-legged on towels drinking coffee and fishing pebbles out of kids' mouths while venting about crazy mornings. They're found in eating the sandwich, opening the door to that bathroom stall, and engaging with life.

Whatever it is that's weighing on you, I challenge you to set it down. You're carrying too much, friend. Give yourself permission like Aubree gave me. Just be you. You're enough.

STEP ONE: Break Up with Perfectionism

The pull of perfectionism shows up differently for everyone. It can look like:

- Lying awake at night analyzing every single thing you did and said, wishing you could have a do-over.
- Negative self-talk: *Why am I such an idiot? I'm a failure. I suck at _____.* You would never speak to anyone the way you speak to yourself.
- Wishing for a personality transplant. If you're loud, wishing you were more mellow. If you're quiet, wishing you were loud.
- Registering other people's strengths as shame in your weakness. For example, when you see that someone is amazing at decorating their house, rather than appreciating it, you find yourself thinking, *Crap, why am I so bad at this?*
- Feeling sure that no matter what you achieve, it's never enough. Having a hard time feeling proud.
- Assuming it's your fault anytime anything goes wrong. *If I had just tried harder, if I just hadn't made that mistake, if I just was better at _____, this never would have happened.*
- Intense stress over seemingly small things.
- Believing your life and happiness would be improved if you just did everything better.
- Being hard on other people (because you're hard on yourself).

If any of that resonated with you (or heck, even if it didn't), it's time to actively give yourself permission to be human.

Aubree told me, "I like you when you're fun and when you're not fun."

Be your own Aubree and fill in the blanks:

Hey _____ [your name], I like you when you're

_____ and I like you when you're _____. I

like you both ways.

If imperfection is needed for belonging and purpose, what

flaws can you celebrate today?

If you're ready, find a trusted friend or family member and

share with them something you're embarrassed about or a

struggle you're wrestling with. It's helpful and healing to get it

out of your head.

LIE #2: I Have to Keep Up with the Kardashians and Also My Neighbor Tammy

Dear God,

I'm not sure if you realize this, but I am a very slow runner.

Like I've had an old lady speed-walk past me while I was jogging, I am not joking.

This is concerning on a variety of levels.

Was there a reason you gave me the motor of a lawn mower? Because I'm tall for a girl, God. I probably could have used a V-8, ya know?

Is there a recall? An aftermarket upgrade?

It might be the cankles that are an issue. Just a thought.

Get back to me on this.

Love,

Jess

I roll over and reach for my phone. I really shouldn't look at it first thing in the morning, but I need to know the time. Seven-twenty. I breathe a sigh of relief—ten more minutes—and fall back on my pillow. But instead of resting or going back to sleep, I start scrolling.

Within twenty seconds, I can feel stress come over me like someone passed gas in the car and all the windows are rolled up.

Look at all these people doing all these things. Look at them just over there winning at life.

My thumb hovers over a girl I knew in high school. She has so many cool tattoos. I feel like I'm a full-sleeve person on the inside. Maybe I should get one. Wow, her vacation looks incredible. I never thought of hiking in Italy, but now I'm thinking about it. How does one even shave enough to wear that swimsuit? Wait, she competes in triathlons? Nice.

My husband breaks my Insta-trance by peeking around the door. "You up?"

> ME: I don't have time for all of this. [I toss my phone like a hot potato.]
> HIM: All of what?
> ME: Thissss. [I flail my hands wildly.]

He does not even understand that this day was already busy with what I had going on and now I have to find a tattoo artist, start hiking, shave my butt, and do a triathlon.

> ME: I don't have time to train for a triathlon.
> HIM: . . .

Sometimes I have a hard time staying in my own lane, especially if I'm particularly unimpressed with my lane at that moment (like in the morning, when I know my next big, exciting activity is going to be scrambling eggs and desperately searching the house for my kid's socks). I don't know if I should say this out loud, but sometimes my life is a little boring, so I get distracted by someone else's life and then I get stressed out because their life also seems hard to achieve.

My lane is where my peace is, I know that, it's just that it's also where the laundry and the dishes are. I'm working on it.

No one is better at staying in his own lane than my dad, Chuck.

When my dad was little, his grandpa leased an old hunting cabin in an off-grid town in Northern California. Dad fell in love with it, and when my brother and I were little, our family moved there.

The cabin was at the end of a long, dusty driveway. The walls were made of lodgepole from the same exact land, and if you looked closely you could see through the cracks between the logs where the chinking had crumbled and fallen out. When the sun shone through the old French-pane windows, you could see billions of particles of dust dancing in the air. I'd sit on the red velvet couch with worn-out arms and stare, wondering if the cloud could be from fairies or angels or something. When my uncle said it was all of our dead skin cells, that made it less magical.

During the day, we'd walk down the driveway to the swimming hole. My mom would sit in the shade with her hat and chair, and my dad would dive in in his cutoff jean shorts. He'd always say something like, "The only way to get in the water is jump in." That was a part of the Chuck Cushman bible, along with, "Ketchup does not go on steak."

My parents started a church in the community center when I was five. It consisted of exactly eleven souls: three old people, another family that came when they could, a woman who made quilts, and her ten-year-old nephew who had "the tapeworms." I knew he had tapeworms because she told us she'd taken a flashlight to the toilet after he used it, and they were all over the place. I tried hard not to sit by her nephew for Sunday school, which was complicated since it was usually just three of us.

The church wasn't glamorous, but my dad loved his job. He treated that town as though it was his church, and when the townspeople realized he was there without expectation or agenda, many of them began to think of him as their honorary pastor even if they had no plans of coming on a Sunday. He rented an office next to the bar—a double-wide with a rickety addition. The bar patrons would sometimes end their shift with a visit to what they called the "drive-up pastor window," a glass slider that went from my dad's desk to the dusty parking lot. They'd stand outside and discuss their thoughts on religion and the height of the river that year. They called my dad "the Rev." My dad loved it. It was his favorite office he'd ever had.

Sometimes when he was around other pastors at a conference somewhere, they'd ask him questions like how many members he had in his church and what programs he offered. They were speechless when he explained that he had eleven members and no programs. I think he enjoyed their shock.

What they didn't understand, and what I could tell, even as a kid, was that my dad was living his best life, one that was full of purpose. The town was his church, and loving the person in front of him was his lane. If someone went to the hospital (an hour's drive away), he was there. If someone got sick, he was visiting. If someone was going through a crisis, he was on it, no questions asked. He was completely present on the path that had him riding in the back of pickup trucks to the top of mountains for tribal burials and holding hands with a mother and father in the hospital while they said goodbye to their child.

There was no reason for him to be concerned with how many people came through the church doors unless he thought that a megachurch was his destination, and he knew that it wasn't.

Peace and purpose don't necessarily come in impressive packages. Actually, in my experience they rarely do. For me, most days they look like making breakfast and gulping down coffee in my oversized T-shirt while the kids ask me if I know where that permission slip went (I do not). They look like picking up shredded pieces of foam ball that the puppy left all over the living room, and they look like sitting in my bed under the covers in my jeans typing because my house is drafty. I don't always feel excited about the day-to-day mundane (sometimes I lose myself down a rabbit hole of Instagram escapism), but I know deep down it's where I'm supposed to be.

In my work, I've learned to stay in my own lane by not taking on every project or job just because the opportunity is presented. That's scary sometimes, because I have the most intense case of FOMO of everyone I know. If a friend calls me up and says, "Hey I'm running to Target, want to come?" I have an existential crisis turning her down, even if I have zero time to join her. What if the dollar section is especially lit? What if she and I were about to have the best conversation ever?

"And I thought we could stop for burgers before heading home."

"Yes. Absolutely yes, I'm in."

When I started sharing my words publicly, someone offered me a job as a staff writer at a bigger publication. It was an honor to be offered, and the FOMO was real. What if this was my one shot? What if doors like this didn't open again? What if . . . what if . . . what if . . . but in my gut, I knew I needed to keep writing for myself and see where it took me. I knew that between diaper changes, trips to the playground, and making endless snacks, I had very little time to invest in pursuing my dream of writing, and I knew I had to be intentional.

In motherhood, too, it's always been a struggle to stay in my lane. I think it's because I want to get it right so badly, and I always think I'm doing it wrong. I've tried on a dozen different parenting methods, but the one that works best for me is being myself and doing the things that feel right for me and my family.

Listen, I know it's hard. Envy sneaks up on you like when they play 2000s hits at the grocery store. The music just kinda takes over my body and all of a sudden I'm in aisle 9 reliving my clubbing days and my kids are all screaming at me to stop. I have no desire to stop grocery-store dancing (sorry, kids), but envy is a different kind of muscle memory I don't want to keep re-creating. I find it so easy to gauge myself by the people around me. But when I find myself spiraling while looking up personal trainers and Groupons to Italy, I've learned that if I re-center myself, I can feel it deep in my chest like a giant sigh of relief. I know when I'm where I belong, and I think you do, too.

I have a friend who is so passionate about homeschooling, she can't help but try to convince her friends and family to try it. One day, we were out in her garden while she got some carrots for dinner. I'd told her that the idea of homeschooling completely stressed me out. "Oh, Jess," she said. "It doesn't have to be stressful!" She gushed about the curriculum she was using. "It's so fun and it's not hard at all. Yesterday we made the alphabet out of bread dough, and then this morning we went outside and made all the letters out of tree branches."

I grinned at her. "I love that you love it," I said, "and I'd rather have my five-year-old cut my bangs than make capital *A*'s out of bread dough." She laughed. Neither of us was wrong. She needs to stay in her lane, and I need to stay in mine.

I used to have a recurring dream about the coffee drive-thru I worked at through high school. In the dream, there would be a line of ten cars on either side and I'd be the only one working. I could see my customers waiting impatiently in their cars as I poured shots. For some reason, my hands wouldn't move quickly. I was stuck in slow motion; I'd try to go faster but I couldn't. The car to the right would order twelve large drinks and I'd frantically (albeit at a snail's pace) pour shots and steam milk. Finally, the last one would be done, and as I turned to get their money, I'd graze the lid with my hand and a twenty-four-ounce quad mocha breve would spill across the counter, knocking over two other drinks on its way down. Then I'd wake up in a sweaty panic because everyone, even my favorite customer, Bob, was mad at me.

That's what it feels like when I stop focusing on what's ahead and get distracted by what others are achieving around me. I think, *Oh crap, should I be doing that, too,* or, *Oh crap, I should be homeschooling and making letters out of bread,* or, *Oh crap, Marie Kondo wants me to figure out which pair of my decade-old underwear brings me joy.* It's what happens when I forget who I am and what I'm called to do. When I get off track, it feels like I'm wearing ice skates to go running.

My path still has challenges and things to overcome, but I have the strength and bandwidth to do those tasks because I know they're mine to do. If I'm confused about my next steps, I slow down (it's more important that I head in the right direction than it is that I get there quickly) and ask myself what my motivation is. Is my motivation fear? Fear of missing out? Fear of letting someone down? Is it guilt? Competitiveness? Envy?

I don't know what you're called to, but I'm guessing that if you get quiet and check your heart, you do.

Maybe it's growing your own food and canning thousands of jars of peaches. Maybe it's starting one of those cat cafés where people just hang out with cats (I will not be coming there, but I think it's cool for you). Maybe it's making waves with a nonprofit that is dear to your heart. Maybe it's getting your own health under control. Maybe it's taking time to pause and rest because you're not sure where your path is headed right now, and rather than just running anywhere, you want to run somewhere.

Maybe for you it *is* competing in triathlons, homeschooling, and Marie-Kondo-ing your underwear drawer.

Make no mistake, every single path includes a whole lot of normal, and sometimes that's really boring. It's not all fancy or exciting for anyone, I promise. Everyone wakes up in a bad mood sometimes. Everyone puts on pants and gets stomach bugs. Everyone wrestles with comparison. If you're scrambling a bowl of eggs and shouting at your kids to please-for-the-love-get-out-of-bed, and you're like, *What am I doing with my life?*— that doesn't mean you're doing it wrong, it means you're doing it, go you.

Right now my path looks like loving my people really, really well (even when it's messy and I have to apologize a lot). It looks like writing and sharing what's in my heart. It looks like sitting on my couch watching funny shows with my teenagers and rubbing their necks and heads when they ask me to. It looks like cooking an exorbitant amount of food for said teenagers and the four other people in my house (and all the extras they bring home). It looks like making intentional time to dream with my husband about the future. It looks like engineering the most ideal throw pillow/blanket situation for my two couches and one chair (and going to HomeGoods regularly, because that is work that's never done). It looks like time with a few special friends. It looks like renting for now. It looks like going camping instead of big fancy trips. It looks like church being in my running shoes on the beach with Maverick City blasting on my headphones.

You know what? When I look at my lane (the real one, not the one I imagine), it looks good. It looks real good. I may get exhausted, I may get bored, but the truth is I wouldn't change it. I'm already sad about the day my kids no longer want me to fold their burrito or drive them to school. Sometimes I get distracted by shiny reels and impressive posts, but there's not a vacation in the world I would trade for these moments, however unglamorous they may be. I'm at home in my heart, right smack dab in the middle of my own journey. Some things will shift and change, but they'll change at the pace that's right for my family.

I can't exactly chuck my phone off a cliff (although I feel like doing it sometimes), but I can set it aside in the evenings when we're watching a movie and pay attention to the way my kids laugh. I can put it down in the morning when I'm already charged with anxious energy and rest my eyes for a few more minutes instead. I can leave it at home when we're at a friend's house for dinner, because this is the good stuff in life and I don't want to waste these moments being distracted. When I feel the feeling of rushrushrush, I can resist, tap the brakes, and breathe. When I'm scrolling and comparing, I can check myself and remember there's only one lane for me, and sometimes the scenic, slow, and potholed route is the very best route.

My friend, stay in your lane. It's where you belong. Don't over-complicate it. You have an important life to live—don't let it be undermined by someone else's. Your lane is just the right place for you. Be proud and stand tall. You look good where you belong.

STEP TWO: Finding Your Lane

If you're not sure what your lane is, take a minute to quiet yourself and ask yourself: *What do I know I'm supposed to be doing right now?*

Make a list with three categories:

1. Things I know I'm meant to do.
2. Things I'm not sure I'm supposed to do.
3. Things that are not mine to do.

If you're unsure, ask yourself: *What is motivating me to do this thing?* Things like guilt, FOMO, shame, envy, and stress are all powerful motivators, but those feelings aren't going to lead you where you want to go.

Now, throughout the week, keep noticing what feels right and good for this season. Keep writing those things down.

Are you feeling any outside pressure to be doing something else? Where is that coming from?

What can you do to re-center yourself and stay focused on your own path?

Don't buy into the lie that you have to keep up or blend in. Your lane is the perfect path for you. Don't look around you. Don't worry if you're moving slow while everyone else is moving fast. Don't stress that no one else seems to struggle with that one thing you struggle with. Don't compare someone else's successes with yours. Don't sweat it if it seems that everyone you know is on a five-lane freeway and you're going ten miles per hour on a dirt road with no reception. This is your life. You are unique and different from every other person. There's only one lane you belong in, and it's yours.

LIE #3: They Forgot My Name Again, and I Think I Might Actually Be Invisible

3/04/2012

Dear Diary,

Went to Starbucks today and they asked me my name. I said Jess.

Almost didn't get my drink because they kept yelling for Jeff.

If my name is Jeff, I'm really going to need to work on my stache.

Jeff for sure has a stache and rides a longboard to work.

I'll be whoever you want me to be, Starbucks, it's fine.

Love,

Jess

One day, someone wrote to me on the internet. They had seen one of my posts that went viral, and they were really upset about the picture I used of Haven and me sleeping. Graham took it a few years ago when he got up to go to work. She had crawled into the bed in the middle of the night and was squished up against me with her hair spread all over the pillow and her chubby hand on my arm. It's one of my favorite pictures of motherhood.

Anyway, they wrote to tell me that they didn't appreciate me using their photo. They demanded to know where I even got this picture of them sleeping with their daughter. They wanted me to know that it was entirely inappropriate for me to go around posting pictures of other people sleeping. I couldn't agree more, that sounded very inappropriate.

I was pretty confused, so I scrolled down to the next message. It was from the same woman's uncle, who really didn't feel okay about me using a picture of his niece and grandniece and demanded I take it down. I scrolled down to find five more messages from aunts, parents, and cousins. *Wow, what a loyal family,* I thought.

It's a particularly weird task, figuring out how to tell someone a picture is not of them or their daughter, but they seemed to take it well. They said, "Oh, sorry . . ." I hoped the daughter's feelings weren't hurt that her whole family apparently couldn't distinguish her from a stranger.

For some reason, God decided to give me one of those faces that looks a lot like other people's faces. People rarely remember me, but they almost always think I remind them of someone they met one time, and have I ever lived in Spain? I have always felt forgettable. I'm the one people don't remember, the one they introduce themselves to three or four times. I've always felt like someone who blends in instead of belonging, like a wallflower in a life I want to dance in.

In high school, I had a best friend with red curly hair. Every time we had Mr. A as a substitute teacher in math class, he would say to her, "Hi, Bethany, how are you?" Then he would turn to me. "Hello, I'm Mr. A, what's your name?"

"Jessica," I'd say, smiling, knowing we'd have this same exchange again the following week.

I am constantly meeting people like Mr. A, and I'm not really sure there's an experience that makes me feel more insignificant.

I remember them. I remember that they're married and have a son in college. I remember that they work at the hospital and they've lived in the same house for twenty years. They don't remember I exist.

I always assumed it was just me, but it turns out most of us feel invisible sometimes.

Of course it's never personal. We all have a lot going on. But because I spent a lot of my life believing that I didn't matter, the moments when people forgot who I was served to confirm my fear.

Another recurring dream I had (yeah, I guess I get those a lot) was that I was in some kind of dangerous situation, and when I tried to scream, nothing would come out. It was just a dream— one I was happy to wake up from. But deep down, I think I was scared (and still sometimes am) that no one could hear me and no one could see me.

The thing about believing you're insignificant is that you start acting like it. You're like the little kid who plops down in the T-ball outfield to pick dandelions because you already know a ball is never making it out there anyway (hi, that was me). You start believing that it doesn't matter if you show up to that party, because no one will notice you're there. You start believing it's not a big deal if you introduce yourself to that person or say hi, because deep down you don't think they'd enjoy the conversation. You start wondering why you feel like an outsider, not realizing you took yourself out of the equation. That's why I think *seeing people* is one of the greatest gifts we can give.

In fifth grade, I started school in the river town where my dad planted his church. I'll never forget showing up the first day in brown corduroy overalls with a brand-new lunch box full of crackers and cheese. No one fell through the cracks at that school (it was hard to when there were only twenty-one students in kindergarten through the eighth grade). I sat down at a long table with my new friends and opened my Tupperware. The cook named Rosie wore an apron as she came out to greet me. "Oh, honey," she said, "don't bother bringing food from home. Everyone eats here." She offered me a plate with homemade bread and lasagna. "Why don't you save that for later." She saw me and invited me in, and as small as it probably seemed to her, it mattered to me.

. When we moved twice three years later and landed in a town where the high school had more than two thousand kids, I felt like I was drowning. I was just a face, just a body taking up space, just one awkward teenager in a herd of teenagers. There were a few people who took the time to notice, offering me a lifeline I was in desperate need of. One was the woman who ran the writing center. She encouraged me in my creative writing process, letting me know she saw me and heard me. She even worked with me and my writing teacher to publish a poem in a statewide anthology. When it got accepted, they both reminded me that I was now a published author and always would be. Their belief in me made me start to believe in myself—to believe that not only was I not invisible, but I had something to say. It was them, along with the couple of friends I made my senior year, that left a lasting impression on my life.

Ten years later, that time would be a faded memory. I was married with three kids under five, and even though I spent most days feeling stressed and overwhelmed, I was happy and my heart was full. I worked part-time at the best coffee shop in town, which was a social outlet as well as a creative one. I loved connecting with the regulars, I loved chatting with my co-workers, and I loved perfecting my latte art. The reclusive girl from high school was long gone. Oaklee, my third baby, was only three months old. Every few hours I'd feel the rush of my milk coming down, and I'd dive behind the counter and sink my thumbs into my nipples to stop the milk from making me look like a double water-balloon victim. (If you don't know that trick, you're welcome.)

The job was a nice break from what my sister-in-law calls the "constant-constant" of motherhood. I rarely found time to write anymore, but I still wondered if I had something to say.

I'd always thought I'd write a book. I didn't know how or what about, but the dream would occasionally get restless and poke at me from somewhere deep down. I borrowed my mom's *Writer's Market 2000* book to try to answer the question *How do I get published?*, but the details of searching out an agent and publisher overwhelmed me in a way that changing diapers and handing out snacks didn't. That was overwhelming, too, but in some ways simpler. I was sniffing things to see if they smelled like pee, searching for the baby's favorite paci, and getting shredded cheese off the floor, which uses a different kind of energy. It was mind-numbing, exhausting, and relentless—but at the same time doable. Finding an agent and publisher? That felt simply impossible. I slammed the book closed after a couple of days, sighed defeatedly, and resigned myself to the fact that I was probably never going to find a way to publish a whole book.

One day a man came into the coffee shop, and I recognized him as one of the janitors at my high school. He had always been kind, and I knew he was married to the woman who worked in the writing center. As I made his double mocha, I asked him if he'd worked at the high school. "Yes, still do," he said with a smile. I could tell he wanted to remember me, but this was ten years after graduation, and the blank look in his eyes when he searched my face told me he didn't.

I told him I remembered his wife from the writing center. He asked my name and told me he'd see if she remembered me (I doubted she would). He took the time to ask me about my life, and I could tell he really listened. When he left, I couldn't help but feel some redemption. I'd encountered my past but with fresh freedom and confidence. It reminded me how grateful I was for my present.

The next Friday, he came back when we were slammed with customers. The line reached nearly out the door. My co-worker and I were in perfect rhythm. She pulled shots and I steamed milk, and we chatted happily with people as they waited. After ordering his drink, the man stood by the counter as I carefully kissed the top of the milk with the steam wand and lowered it deep to create a perfect whirlpool of whole milk. "Hey," I said cheerfully, "how are you today?"

"I'm good," he said. Then as I finished pouring and gently moved my wrist to finish a rosette at the top of his sixteen-ounce cup, he said, "I asked my wife about you."

I slid the cup toward him, surprised. "Really?" I asked.

"Really," he said deliberately, and then he looked into my eyes and said something I'll never forget. "She remembers you." He pointed his finger at me like he was about to say something important. "She remembers you, and she remembers your work, and she told me to tell you that you need to keep writing."

His words pierced straight to my heart. I suddenly felt vulnerable and small. I thought I'd grown up since I last saw him. I thought I'd arrived. I was a (mostly) well-adjusted adult, a mom of three, a person who I thought had found her voice, but the truth was, I still didn't know that my voice was of any value. I still didn't know that my dream was worth pursuing. I thought I'd shaken off all remnants of the invisible girl from high school, but I hadn't.

"She remembers you, and you need to keep writing" pulled me from chaos and told me I had something to offer the world.

It told me my voice was not only heard but significant, and the dream that was growing restless was worth paying attention to.

Listen, I don't know if someone will come into your life and offer you a lifeline like that. I hope they do, but even if they don't, I want to tell you something: You matter, you are memorable. Who you are in this world has never been seen before and will never again be repeated. No one will sing the song you were created to sing, whatever that may be. Maybe you really are musical, maybe you love to cook, maybe you're a businesswoman, maybe you paint, maybe you're a mother, maybe you're a person who works at a high school and takes the time to actually see your students. What is the version of *You need to keep writing* that you need to hear?

You need to keep _____, *because you are significant and who you are matters.*

Keep showing up, keep speaking up, keep using your gifts, keep being creative, heck, keep re-introducing yourself to people you've already met.

You matter. Even with billions of people on this planet, you matter, and your contribution matters. You matter in the day-to-day things, like your interactions with your Uber driver and the elderly lady you held the door open for at the grocery store. You matter in your circles of influence. Even if there are five hundred parents represented at your kid's elementary school, getting involved and using your voice matters. Don't let the BS keep you small for one minute longer, and if you need encouragement like I did that day, let this be it. Nothing about you was a mistake. Nothing about you is unimportant. The world and your people need you to create what you were meant to create and be who you were meant to be.

I promise it's the truth. Take it from a wallflower who is still meeting people she's already known for a decade or more.

There will always be things in life that try to convince you to stay small and stay quiet. I don't know what or who caused you to feel insignificant, but I am certain that it's happened. Maybe you were raised to believe it was your job to keep the peace at home and make the important people in your life happy. You've followed those expectations, and that impossible job has caused your own needs and desires to shrivel. Maybe you've gotten negative feedback for having too many opinions, talking a lot, or being too much. You're constantly trying to rein yourself in, and it's exhausting. I don't know what your particular messages are or what things are trying to squash you, but I do know this: lies, all of it.

I'm a writer now, but I sometimes still wonder if I have anything important to say. The difference is that now I know not to pay attention to the self-doubt. I just write anyway. I've learned that the best way to manage a lie like that is by putting one foot in front of the other. Often the best way to stop believing a lie is to ignore it, if not with your mind, then by your actions.

I defy the lies every time I eat a big meal and savor every bite. (Looking at you, eating disorder.)

I defy the lies when I share my opinions.

I defy the lies when I'm tormented by them, but then I get out of bed in the morning and make breakfast for my family, and I sit down to brush my daughter's hair.

I defy the lies when I go to the party, even though I'm in a storm of depression and I'm struggling to believe that I matter.

I defy the lies every single time I choose to live big, live freely, and take up space.

The most powerful action we can take to defy the lies is to intentionally notice people and let them know they matter. We can be the writing teachers and lunch ladies of the world, lighting flames everywhere we go. Rather than waiting to be seen, we can make sure we see the people around us, giving them an invitation to engage. I see you, I remember you, you're not invisible to me.

My friend Amy compliments an elderly woman every time she goes grocery shopping. She stops them in the bread aisle or the produce department and says, "Excuse me, but I just needed to tell you that you have the most beautiful eyes," or "I couldn't help but notice your jacket today, it's stunning." They light up every single time, because gosh, it's such a gift to be seen.

Life is busy, but it only takes a second to notice the people around us. We don't have to notice everyone, but we can notice the person in front of us in the coffee line, or the one beside us at the gym. My kids tease me because I am always stopping people in the coffee shop to tell them I love their shoes, or their purse, or their nails. It's a small thing. It only takes a second. But it matters.

If you're at the park and you see a mom on her knees talking to her tantruming toddler and you think, *Wow, what a good mom,* tell her. Add fuel to her fire, let her know she's doing a great job. If you're at Sephora with your teenage daughter and the saleslady takes extra time and care helping her find the right product, and you think, *Wow, she's good at this,* tell her. If you walk past a woman playing the guitar and singing downtown and you think, *What a beautiful voice,* tell her.

We do this thing where we assume people know if they're doing a good job, or they're talented, or they're a natural at whatever it is they're doing. They don't. And if they do, who cares? Everyone could use a little sprinkling of encouragement on their garden.

Be the kind of woman who sees other women, be the kind of person who sees other people, because I don't think there's a single other thing that will make you feel less insignificant.

STEP THREE: Believe That You Matter (Even If People Forget Your Name)

No really, my friend, you do. It's imperative that you know that.

Get out your journal and jot down a few things that make you you. Not just the things you think of as good or important but the things that are unique, messy, and silly, too.

I'll start:

I am more creative than I am organized. I read somewhere that messy people are just so creative, we think of new places to put things all the time. Why be held back by a single drawer when you can try out a new home for your stuff every single time?

I have excessively thick hair, and the back of my hairline runs onto my neck, where it turns into peach fuzz.

I love people deeply.

I'm a noticer and oftentimes a starer because I love to soak in people with all their nuances.

I have very little rhythm, but I love music and I love to dance.

I'm a writer, and I was a writer even before I ever wrote a single thing that was published.

What's your list?

LIE #4: I'm Going to Need to Shrink, Suck It All In, Quiet Down, and Possibly Disappear

05/30/2007

Dear Diary,

I tried on a dress in the fitting room at Target today. It looked too small, to be honest, but the endorphins from the candle aisle lingered, and I had the faith to move mountains and shrink thighs. I had just finished breastfeeding and the baby was gurgling, so I had five minutes to fit myself into this human condom, tops.

I sweated a lot to get into that thing, mostly because I kept having to rescue the paci off the ground and clean it. Once I had it over my shoulders, I realized something awful: I couldn't put my arms down. One arm was above my head like I was moshing at a concert and the other was kind of trapped against my body. That's when I started to panic, because what do you do when you've imprisoned yourself in a dress at Target?

I sat there staring at myself in the mirror all red-faced and sweaty, thinking, *Well, I guess this is where it ends, because I'm not inviting William in the red shirt to help me.*

After some sweating and groaning and wondering if William might grab me a stick of butter, I finally got it off. But let me tell you, it was a close one.

All clothes should be stretchy. All dresses should have zip-
pers. Small, tight dresses are overrated. I am an idiot.

Love,

Jess

I t was a fall day at Etna Elementary School. I was having a good
bangs day, and I'd just been moved to be desk partners with
the cutest boy in class. My life as a second grader had reached the
pinnacle of greatness. The only thing I didn't love was being the
tallest girl, bested only by a boy named Sam who kept telling
me I was his girlfriend (because dating was generally decided by
whoever was closest in height). I told him I believed in lepre-
chauns, hoping to scare him away, but it didn't. He listened pa-
tiently to my story about catching a leprechaun the night before,
then he said he loved me.

We were all at our cubbies, putting away our writing books,
when Mrs. S asked for our attention. We stopped the zipping of
our backpacks and turned. "Class," she said, "PE has been can-
celed for today. Instead, we're going to have an extra free-play
computer day this week."

I was overcome with joy. In just a few short minutes, I would
be setting off on a fresh journey on the Oregon Trail.

I don't know what happened exactly, but somehow, this pure
ecstasy took over my body, and my shy self was shoved aside
momentarily by the boisterous person I would become. I let out
a bloodcurdling scream, right there in the classroom. I think I
expected everyone else to do the same. How could one not
scream when the Oregon Trail was just minutes away? Except
no one screamed or even clapped or even cheered. Just me. Just
me letting it all out like I was whooping in a rodeo or yodeling in
the Swiss Alps. The emotion was joy. The noise was . . . question-

able. Was I being stabbed? Seeing a ghost? Winning a brand-new car on *The Price Is Right*? One could not be sure.

Halfway through the scream, I realized that the room was dead quiet. My teacher looked up from her desk, and her wide eyes met mine. "Please keep it down," she said.

The embarrassment I felt in that moment, not even the Oregon Trail could distract me from.

Here's what I learned that day: *Keep it locked down, Jess. Don't be extra, or you're going to make everyone uncomfortable. Be happy, but don't, like, freak out. Be friendly, but not so outgoing it's weird. Be sad (if you must), but don't let anyone see you cry (because you're not a cute crier, and all that snot is gross). Anger is a no for sure; no one wants to see that. Be confident, but don't do anything you're not already sure you're good at (because what if you look dumb?). And for the love don't ever stand out (even for good things), because then people might talk about you.*

I have always felt the need to shrink myself. Maybe it was the way I was always the tallest, maybe it went all the way back to ballet class, or maybe it was before that, in Sunshine Nursery School, when I wanted to play Baby Jesus in the Christmas play, but Katy said she would have to play him because I was way too big and she was tiny and cute. (We were all disappointed to find out Baby Jesus would actually be played by a Cabbage Patch doll.) Maybe it was when I watched rom-coms as a teenager and was always struck by the tininess of the heroine's butt, the thinness of her arms, the delicateness of her ankles. Maybe it was when I learned that some people became the brunt of jokes, and some people made the jokes, and I just wanted to be accepted by the joke-making people. When I did stand out, it was usually for something embarrassing, like getting poison oak on my face, or screaming in second grade, or turning bright red for the two hours after PE.

Do you ever just want to shrink yourself? Like, let me just slip into the shadows and hopefully people forget I'm here. Have you ever worried you are too much? Like, if I let these emotions out of the vault people are going to say, "No thank you, you're scaring me."

It reminds me of when Graham and I were dating and he thought it was weird that I never farted around him. He came from a free-farting family. I came from a family that didn't believe in farts (not just "We don't fart around others"—but also "We don't acknowledge that farts exist").

He was always trying to get me to let one go, but I did not. He, on the other hand, farted constantly. He farted under the stars, farted in the car, and farted in the silence between songs on the radio. The only place he didn't fart was at my parents' house, after which he always complained of being very bloated.

Apparently he thought my gas was going to smell like jasmine and orange blossoms or something, because when I finally let one out, he was horrified. We have been married almost eighteen years and he is still surprised my farts smell bad.

When I fart, he acts as though I have physically assaulted him. He grabs his face, his eyes start watering, and he demands "WAS THAT YOU???!!!!"

"Yes."

"OH MY GOD WHY IS IT SO BADDDDD!!!!????"

"Because I am a human person."

"SOMETHING DIED IN YOUR INTESTINES!!!!"

"Welcome to my world," I say calmly. Maybe in this unique instance, Graham does wish I kept it locked down and hiding in the shadows.

Don't worry, we don't need to fart for everyone. But if you've been trying to shrink into the background of your family, your friend group, or your workplace, ask yourself why. Is it because you know deep down your gas smells bad?

(*Kidding,* sorry, moving on.)

I spent the first two decades of my life trying to shrink. I did it so desperately and for so long that by the time I realized it, I no longer knew how to take up space.

It's not that we don't see women expressing themselves on-stage or taking up space in conference rooms, or that we don't admire them. It's that we're really not sure what would happen if we walked up on that stage. Would people listen? Would they wonder why we had the audacity to climb up? To some of us, it seems much safer to stay small than to be noticeable. The pretty girls, the desirable ones, have tiny bodies and perfect voices, and they don't say dumb things. And if they do take a misstep, God help them. We watch those women get humiliated and shamed by the same people who once praised them, and it reinforces our instinct to shrink. We always knew deep down it was that way, but this proves it.

In Australia and New Zealand, they call the idea that we shouldn't take up too much space or draw too much attention Tall Poppy Syndrome (the tallest poppy will get cut down). In Japan, they say, "The nail that sticks up gets hammered down." In the Philippines, it's been called Crabs in a Bucket Syndrome: If an individual crab tries to climb out of the bucket, the other crabs will pull it back down.

I cannot tell you how many times I've dared to share an opinion and then felt embarrassed and longed to take it back. How dare I make someone else uncomfortable by having opinions that challenge theirs?

I cannot tell you how much time I've wasted overthinking things I've shared or said, or jokes I've told that were maybe just a bit too much.

I cannot tell you how often I've chastised myself for losing it emotionally. For falling apart. For not keeping things under wraps.

The truth is, we were meant to take up space. With our bodies, with our ambitions, with our desires, with our appetites, with our voices, with our opinions, and with our emotions.

The second time I met Graham, I told him that snowboarding was my life. We were in a dark club shouting over the Black Eyed Peas. Fueled by hip-hop and two Red Bulls, I gushed like I was one of those girls who lives on the mountain and boards all day every day while only stopping momentarily to eat PB&Js and put a new Linkin Park tape in my Walkman. I told him I couldn't live without it. It was my passion, my vice, my everything. Following my lead, he said we should definitely go together. "Yes!" I exclaimed, so excited. I did not hold back. I did not tone it down.

I just forgot to mention one tiny detail: I did not know how to snowboard. I had gone quite a few times, and I loved the idea of it. I also loved the seconds at a time I was gliding upright. Mostly I loved the french fries in the cafeteria. For some reason those brown eyes and broad shoulders made me check all caution at the door. Graham called me to set a snowboarding date and I just kind of went with it. *I might die,* I thought. *But I also might marry him, so.*

The day came, and what I lacked in skill, I made up for in Avril Lavigne eyeliner and a red trucker hat. The more nervous I felt, the more eyeliner I added. I crossed my fingers that he wouldn't notice the five hours he'd have to wait at the bottom of each slope for me to catch up.

I'm not sure what I thought was going to happen, to be honest, but I'll tell you what did happen. We laughed, we flirted, we went outside, I said something super cute, and then I pointed my board down the slope. I went approximately four feet before I face-planted into the snow. I didn't know what to do, so I just started laughing. I lifted myself up as awkwardly as one does when one's feet are attached to a snowboard, and there I sat, laughing hysterically with black eyeliner streaming down my face, looking like Marilyn Manson instead of Avril Lavigne.

He started laughing, too, and I broke the news to him that maybe I'd forgotten to mention that even though I loved snowboarding, I was really, really bad at it. He said he had noticed that. I've always liked to keep him guessing. I'm the gift that keeps on giving.

P.S. He's always told me that the way I face-planted on that mountain and laughed my head off made him fall more in love with me, so there's that.

Don't take this story the wrong way. I'm not saying exaggerating your abilities and hurling yourself down a mountain is the way to find what you're looking for. I am saying that the dreams in my heart mostly came true when I stopped trying to make myself small and stopped trying to follow rigid guidelines and rules that kept me quiet. When I stepped onto the dance floor. When I ate the big meal without fear of my appetite. When I laughed loudly, bought pants that didn't dig in, whooped when I felt like whooping, and let myself take up space.

It was already a win because I showed up. I didn't stay home in the basement ignoring my hunger pangs and adding up calories on the backs of boxes. I didn't say no to a date because I was afraid of embarrassing myself (again). I went to where the music was, and I let myself be present. I didn't worry about the rules or staying small; I engaged with life. I was alive.

I shrieked when everyone else stayed quiet, so what? I face-planted when all the other girls around me carved gracefully (I'm assuming; I couldn't really see them with all that snow in my eyes)—so what!

Meeting Graham ended the season of floating and anchored me. Graham made space for me to be me—more of me than I'd ever been (even my farts, ha). He was (and is) my ultimate safety.

When I talked, he listened.

When I was angry and ranted about something I didn't like, he didn't get mad; he laughed. Some people might not like that, but I loved that he wasn't scared of me or my big feelings.

When I shared my opinions he was there for it, even if they were different from his own.

When I had big emotions, he didn't run away.

When I shared a dream with him, he told me firmly I could do it.

He thought I was funny.

He thought I was amazing, and the more I let him see my weird quirks and flaws, the more amazing he thought I was.

I know we all don't get the opportunity to meet Grahams. I wish we did, but I do know we can all be that kind of person for someone else, and I know we can be it for ourselves.

This restriction we feel? It's not you and it's not me. It's bigger than that. It's an oppressive paradigm that has been trying to squash women for far too long. It's your aunt coming to visit and talking about her new diet. It's the catalogs we saw as little girls that showed only stick-thin, leggy models. It's the whispers we heard in the hallways: "Yeah she's pretty, but she's a slut." (Meanwhile, the guys are celebrated for the same behavior.) It's the way we see powerful women being labeled as B-words, and men simply as strong leaders.

Nothing makes me want to change it more than thinking about my kids.

I have a daughter who is a force of nature. She's our youngest, and from the day she came into this world, she has made her presence known. She climbed out of every crib before she was ten months old, belted every word to "Hello" by Adele by the time she was two, and threw more tantrums than all my other kids combined by the time she was three.

One summer when she was little, we were at the beach with

friends. It was getting close to the time to go home, so I gave her a ten-minute warning, a five-minute warning, a two-minute warning, and a promise of a pre-nap snack, and then I crossed my fingers and hoped for the best. When the time arrived, no amount of reasoning, reminding, or empathizing helped. She did not want to go, and she was not going to back down. I ended up walking the quarter mile to my car with her in my arms kicking and screaming, all three of my other kids trailing behind us in a parade of shame. I felt like I could melt from the disapproving stares of strangers. My face was red and hot from embarrassment, and I could barely hold in the tears until I got through the door of our house. I lay down with her until she finally fell asleep, and then I bawled.

I remember whispering through my tears:

"I like you. I like your strong will and your loud voice. I like your wild spirit and your fierce heart. I wouldn't change a thing about you."

I brushed the sweaty hair from her cheeks and said, "I will love you, I will guide you, but I will never tame you.

"I will carry you home kicking and screaming as many times as is needed, because, girl, you're going to move mountains. There's nowhere I'd rather be than right here, raising you."

It wasn't my job to quiet her; it wasn't my job to break her spirit. It was my job to help her channel her passion. From then on, the song I sang her at bedtime became, "This little light of mine, I'm going to let her shine."

Nothing gives me more perspective on myself than the way I love my kids. Nothing makes me see myself differently more than the way I see them.

I don't really think that the way to change Tall Poppy Syndrome is just to grow tall. That's part of it, definitely, but I think the bigger part is celebrating the women around us when they grow tall. It's cheering when we see someone use their voice and take up space in a room. It's stopping ourselves before we find fault in the person with the platform or on the stage, and instead saying, *Yes, go you.* It's actively looking for the sparkle and light in our friends and telling them how much we love to see them shine. It's not just me or them; it's all of us. I think what the world needs right about now is to hear a whole lot of women roar.

My daughter is in elementary school now. Just a few days ago she had a singing recital. I watched that fierce and free girl walk onto the stage in a way that commanded it. She doesn't question if she belongs there; she knows she does. She sang her heart out, and my eyes filled with tears. She knows the power of her voice, and she doesn't hold back.

That's what I want for all of us.

STEP FOUR: Stand Tall, Be Noisy, Take Up Space

What is the "thing" about yourself that you think you should shrink?

Is it your personality?

Your thighs?

Your opinions?

Your dreams?

Whatever it is, I promise you're not alone. This isn't a new thing. The first step is recognizing it and calling it what it is: a load of crap. Spread yourself out in your personality, let those thighs be thunderous, let your opinions be unapologetic, and let your dreams break down the walls meant to contain you.

And, friend, pay attention to the people in your life who make room for you to grow and the people who don't. Some will try to keep you small. It might be offhanded comments or criticizing you when you're loud. It might be making general statements about who you are that you know no longer fit you. Maybe you've worked on becoming more generous, say, but they continue to call you selfish. It might be reminding you of things you're trying to let go of, like calories and pant sizes. They probably don't mean to. Maybe they're just unaware, or maybe your noise is making them uncomfortable with their own quietness. Maybe their insecurity feels uncomfortable around your security. Don't be afraid to gently make space between you and the ones who don't have room while you lean into the ones who do. Old friendships and relationships can always come back around. Sometimes you have to take a couple of steps away to grow the way you're supposed to grow.

Whatever those things are for you, we're going to unbutton those way-too-tight jeans and put on a soft pair of sweatpants with a band that stretches for days, because it's time to get bigger. It's time to take up space.

LIE #5: Pretending to Be Fine Is the Same Thing as Being Fine

12/25/2016

Dear Diary,

It's Christmas Day and I have a fever of 105, and I think I just hallucinated the three ghosts of Christmas past.

My kids are opening presents at their grandma's house and eating cake.

I asked Graham for toast before they left. He forgot.

When my eight-year-old asked if I was okay, I said, "Of course! Have fun! I'm fine!"

I have pneumonia, and I can't walk right now. I just mainly crawl around the house trying to hydrate and feed myself. But I'm fine.

I really need my toast . . .

Love,
Jess

If I'm not careful, I have two moods:

Mood 1: I'm great! (I really am great.)

Mood 2: I'm great! (I'm not at all great. I am hanging on by a thread, and my life is in the literal garbage can. Also I have a headache and I can't find pants that don't dig in, and everyone is mad at me, and I don't remember if I sent my third grader their field-trip permission slip, but I'm trying desperately to push through to being great, and maybe if I down this triple latte it will help. So if you could just pretend my smile isn't forced and creepy, we can maintain this delusion together.)

I don't know when or where it happened, but at some point in life, I learned to undermine my own struggle. I learned to grin and bear it. I learned that no one wanted to hear me whine or complain, so it's better to suck it up. Nobody told me this, exactly. I just liked the feedback I got when I was funny and happy, and I didn't like the feedback I got when I was having a hard time. It felt like no one knew what to do. I felt like my issues were bigger than anyone could handle.

I am an Enneagram 7 (the enthusiast). Sevens are restless, impatient, and likely to suggest popping over to Barbados for the weekend if it means we could escape having to do paperwork or go to the dentist. We like fun, a lot of fun. My best friend, Aubree (yep, she's back), always tells me, "You think it's bad to feel uncomfortable things, and it's not." Yes, Aubree, it does feel bad to feel those things. Why would I want to do that when instead we could go shopping and get pedicures and pretend that we are fine?

I have another friend who went through one of the greatest traumas imaginable. The kind where people whisper quietly, *How will she ever come back from this?* She did come back from it. She will never be the same, but she is incredibly powerful and beautiful as she stands in the wreckage of everything she once knew to be true. She is a beacon of hope to me, and she's never been so vibrant and beautiful as she is now.

She and I have similar personalities. She is a seven, too, and she is very familiar with the impulse to be fine when she is not fine. In the process of healing, we had a lot of long conversations—one, in particular, when I was going through some stuff of my own.

"You know," she said, "I've been learning to sit in the pain, and you know what's crazy? It doesn't last forever. It actually passes."

This was mind-blowing to me.

She continued, "When I feel depressed, I let myself feel depressed instead of trying to escape. When I feel sad or off, I just let myself fully feel sad and off. And it lifts, sometimes in a matter of minutes, like a wave that passes over me. When I used to run from it, it would last for days and weeks."

"So," I said, fighting to wrap my mind around this, "you mean rather than getting ice cream, or going shopping, or researching tickets to Hawaii, you just let yourself feel sad?"

"Yes."

"And it passes?"

"Yes."

"Are you sure?"

She laughed, "Yeah, I'm sure."

She and I are familiar with medication for anxiety and depression. (And I'm grateful for it.) We know what it's like to need help rising above the water when we're drowning, and that's not what she's talking about. If the dark days are consuming you, please, please reach out for help. There are absolutely times when you cannot, and should not, navigate the darkness on your own.

But my friend is right about running away from pain.

Sometimes I wish I had a midwife for life. Someone to sit with me when the hard things come up and remind me that it will pass. Some pain is so hard and so intense, it feels like fighting my own human instinct to remain still. It's like birth, where no 1-through-10 pain scales can bring understanding, only swear words and nail gouging your partner's hand. When it came time to push, I screamed, "I can't do it!" and my midwife looked solidly in my eyes and told me I could. She said I was doing amazing, and it was going to be okay. She told me she could see the head and soon my baby would be in my arms. With each contraction and each push, she said it again. It wasn't that I believed her, it was that she believed for me, and somehow that got me through.

Admitting things are hard or broken or messed up is difficult for me. Don't get me wrong, positivity can be an awesome trait, but there is a fuzzy line between positivity and full-on denial (and I dabble).

Maybe you aren't head-in-the-clouds like I am. Maybe you're more rational and less prone to absurd positivity. But is there a pain in your life that you're struggling to face? Do you know that you should probably go to counseling, but you've been putting it off for years? Do you shove down questions that you don't have answers for because it's too dang painful? If so, I get it. It was Brené Brown who said you can't feel the fullness of joy if you don't also feel sadness. You can't be choosy about which emotions you numb. If you numb one, you numb them all.

Aubree, the queen of charging full ahead into the pain, continues to inspire me. I've studied her mysterious ways for the past decade and a half, and I'm still learning (slowly).

If we hung out on a day when I was feeling off, I used to tell her, "I'm not doing good. I'm just not myself."

Until one day she told me, "Jess, you realize this is you, too, right? When you're not doing good, you're still you. This is just a different part of you."

I hated that, and I loved it at the same time.

As I sit with the pain and fight back the urge to run, I'm learning it's not as bad as I thought it would be. When I let myself feel all the things, I walk through them and become a more whole person, a person who is healing. I'm relieved to discover that my feelings don't become my permanent reality. Maybe pieces of them do. But the deep pain? It passes.

I can almost hear what some of you are thinking right now, because I've thought it, too:

I don't have time to not be fine.

You have no idea how much is on my plate right now.

Maybe I'll be not-fine later.

Hey, sister, the world isn't going to stop for you. You're going to have to make it stop.

Sometimes I wake up in the morning, and I know I'm not fine. Grief from loss feels heavy on my soul. My anxiety is through the roof. My to-do list is so long, I'm going to need three of me to just get through it. The not-fine rarely comes when it's convenient.

Just this morning I had therapy, and I brought up something that currently is not fine. I have work deadlines, kids' dentist appointments, and visitors coming in on Thursday for whom I do not yet own a bed (Facebook Marketplace, please do right by me). I've got kids who are basically pygmy shrews who will die if they don't eat three times their body weight each day. I've got a bill I really need to pay and I keep forgetting, I said yes to this random luncheon thing on Wednesday that I never should have said yes to, and so on. Also, all my bras are dirty. Jesus, take the wheel.

I do not have time for this. But I am learning something. I'm learning that I have to take care of my heart, and my heart shouldn't land on the bottom of the list, but the top. We are never, ever going to have time to not be fine, but we're going to have to make that time, because our hearts are the greatest treasure we own.

It's hard when you're struggling with something that you don't think you're supposed to struggle with. Maybe you're in a difficult stage of parenting and having a hard time. You feel like you've lost yourself, and you don't know how to find her again, but when you're out with your kids at the playground or at the grocery store, people stop you and say, "Isn't it wonderful? Enjoy every single second, it goes by so fast." You feel shame because you're not enjoying every single second. In fact, you're simply surviving a lot of seconds. You try to stuff the struggle down further, but it doesn't go away. You wonder what is wrong with you. You know you'll miss these days, but you're still not okay. Then, one day you meet up with a friend who has kids the same age. She confides in you that she's wrestling with the transition into motherhood. She tells you that she's finding the sleepless nights really hard, and you find yourself getting emotional. Her acknowledgment of the hard of motherhood is exactly what you need right now. She's set the table for truth, and you tell her that you understand what she's going through, and you tell her some of your hard.

Or maybe you've just gotten married and everyone tells you this is the "best year of all the years" and isn't it magical? But you've actually been having a really hard time with the transition. You don't want to be ungrateful, but you feel trapped in overwhelming feelings you didn't expect. Finally you share the truth with a trusted someone, and she puts her hand on your shoulder and says, "Oh, honey, my first year of marriage was the hardest." Suddenly you're a little bit freer.

Maybe you've achieved a big goal or dream, and instead of feeling on top of the world, you feel down in the dumps. People who don't get it tell you things like, "You should be grateful," or "Just focus on the positive." Eventually you open up to your therapist and she explains to you that it's called post-achievement depression or arrival fallacy, and it's totally normal. Common, even.

Sometimes you need to just say it's hard. Parenting is hard. Marriage is hard. Life is hard. It doesn't mean it's all hard or that it's not also good.

Find people in your life who know how to handle the messy truth. People who don't gloss over it or tell you to just cheer up. People who are encouraging, but also let you know that they see you and you're not crazy or dramatic. Find those people and be that person for them, too.

If someone opens up to you about their hard, listen and hold space. You don't have to have experienced it to let them know that you see them and it makes sense they'd feel that way. Practice putting yourself in other people's shoes. Say your honeymoon was the best thing that ever happened. You were living your actual magical fairy tale. Sex was great, weather was perfect, nothing was awkward or weird. You were in the fraction of the month unaffected by PMS or cramping, and you had zero moodiness or unpleasant emotions. Then your friend comes home from her honeymoon, and she tells you that it was the trip from hell. When they arrived, they found out they'd accidentally booked their trip in monsoon season; her bikini never left the suitcase. She and her new husband fought more than they ever had, and one night they both got food poisoning and were privy to smells and sounds they would never be able to unsmell or unhear. Half of their honeymoon she had raging PMS, and she was flooded with unexpected anxiety and depression. She was so disappointed, but she was embarrassed to tell anyone because everyone assumed that she'd had the best time ever.

You can't relate through your own experience, but you can relate by putting yourself in her shoes. Think of a time you dealt with intense anxiety or depression. How did that feel? What would it have been like to try to enjoy your honeymoon while also struggling that deeply? If you haven't dealt with that, it's okay—find something else that does resonate with you. Think of a time when something you'd dreamed about for a long time didn't turn out the way you'd hoped. Imagine how difficult it must be for her to feel like everyone expects a great story when it actually was just really hard.

You can tell her something like this: *It makes complete sense that you'd feel anxious and depressed. Getting married is a huge transition, and it hits everyone differently. I'm so sorry you dealt with that. That must have been incredibly difficult to navigate.*

Once you've heard her, sat with her, and validated her, ask her if she could use some encouragement. If so, this is when you can hit her with all that pent-up positivity (I'm looking at you, fellow Enneagram 7s).

Sometimes the hard is bigger than you, it's bigger than your friends, and it's bigger than your family. The people who love you are invaluable, but they're most likely not trained therapists and don't have all the tools you need. It's not fair to any of you to expect them to be your only recourse when they aren't qualified or trained. I started seeing a therapist (for the second time) four years ago because something came up in my life that was deep-rooted like a thistle. I tried to pull it out, but I couldn't, and when the people who loved me tried to help me, I got triggered and defensive (which was not fun for them).

If that's where you are, my best advice is not to overthink it. Don't get stuck in the weeds of "who should I see?" Ask for a recommendation from a local Facebook group (you can usually post anonymously if you want). Sign up for online counseling. Look into free resources at your church or in your community. Just move one foot in front of the other. My only regret is that I didn't start it earlier.

I take a Yoga Sculpt class sometimes. Yoga Sculpt is not to be confused with the relaxing kind of yoga; it's more of a sweaty, make-it-stop kind. We were doing squats with weights, and I was feeling the burn and wondering if I could discreetly stop but make it look like my ponytail had come undone, when the instructor said something that stuck with me: "Close your eyes and be present in the pain. You'd think it would make it feel like it's taking longer, but it's the opposite. It will make it feel faster. It's funny like that."

Sometimes all it takes is acknowledging it. Sometimes it takes feeling it instead of running from it. Sometimes it takes being seen in our pain. Sometimes it takes taking the plunge and finding a therapist.

My friend, if you've been waiting for a sign to deal with some stuff, this is it.

STEP FIVE: Stop Pretending You're Fine When You're Not Fine

Get out a journal, a notepad, or a random scrap of paper. Now commit to being honest with yourself.

When was the last time you pretended to be fine when you were not fine?

In that moment, why did you feel the pressure to be okay?

How did that leave you feeling?

Is there anything you're struggling with now that you're scared to face?

What can you do about it? Is there someone you can bring into the struggle with you? A friend or a family member you can talk to?

If you twisted your ankle but didn't want to admit it was twisted, so you just kept using it as if it weren't, it wouldn't make the injury any less painful, but it would keep you from being able to heal.

It's okay to stop pushing things down. It's okay to look directly at the things you're wrestling with. Even though it feels like it might swallow you whole, it's not going to. Facing it will allow you to heal.

PART TWO

- - - - - - - - - - - - -

Lies That Keep
Us from Connection

(Or, How to Quit Performing

and Start Belonging)

LIE #6: If I'm Rejected, I Will Die

7/20/2016

Dear Diary,

I texted someone today to see if she wants to get coffee (yay me!).

It's been ten minutes and she hasn't texted back.

It's totally fine.

Update: Okay, it's been an hour, Diary.

Now it's nighttime and I know that she hates me and doesn't know how to let me down nicely.

She's trying to figure out how to say, "I hate you and I never want to have coffee with you," but in a polite way, which would be difficult.

Should I tell her it's okay, she doesn't need to? Is that a weird text?

Update: She texted me this morning and she doesn't hate me. She was just out of service. Haha, false alarm.

We're getting coffee Tuesday.

Love,

Jess

stepped out of the car and looked out at the field filled with parents and kids.

"Mom, do you have my socks?"

"Yeah," I said absentmindedly, handing them over and reaching for my purse.

I followed my son as he bounced ahead through the gate.

Today is the day, I told myself. *Today is the day I make friends with the other parents.*

I glanced up and saw them gathered together. They were so tight. They'd been doing this for years. I was a newbie.

I'm going to walk right over there and say something hilarious. They're going to love me. They're going to be, like, Come sit with us and have some chips.

"Hi," I said, making sure to smile. But I'd said it too soon. I'd pre-hi'd. I was too far away and my words were lost in the space between us, falling unheard on the dewy green sod. The ten of them kept chatting. I didn't have the courage for the second hi. I was hi'd out.

Pull yourself together. You're a full-grown woman. You have friends. You're not shy.

I kept walking toward them and smiled in their direction, but at the last second I veered toward the stands.

Nope, today was not the day. Tomorrow would be a better time to infiltrate the parent crew.

I would rather singe off my eyebrows than risk being rejected, but there's nothing that has gained me more in my life. Every job I've ever gotten, I got by walking through the door and asking if they were hiring. Every friendship I've ever built required risking my heart. I met Graham because I showed up to a twenty-and-under club with my friends even though I was feeling insecure and awkward. When he started dancing with me, I kept dancing even though I'm not actually a great dancer (instead of running away with an excuse like "I need to use the bathroom"). Now we've been married for eighteen years.

When the kids were little, Graham and I lived in a little cookie-cutter house in Montana. Malachi was three and Scout was one. Life was good, but we were lonely. I remember waiting by my phone one weekend for a call because someone had mentioned possibly doing dinner that Saturday. When the call didn't come, I got unreasonably upset. I felt like crying as I started prepping sweet potatoes for our own four-person meal. As I chopped, I analyzed myself. Why was I so upset? I knew I was being irrational. I understood that they weren't rejecting me, they were just busy. Was I about to start my period? Why did I feel so desperate?

I felt stuck in a cycle, like each day was exactly the same. Every night I was up and down with the kids, moving to different beds like a sleep-deprived mombie (mom + zombie). I'd wake up in the morning with a tension headache and someone's feet pressed into my back. Then I'd spend the day changing diapers and making snacks while Graham worked. In the evening, we'd survive a chaotic dinner of spilled cups, spit-out bites, and crumbs that somehow touched every surface. Then we'd tuck them in with rituals that grew longer every night (butterfly kisses, Eskimo kisses, three books, two songs, and a prayer that included every person and animal they'd ever met or seen on TV). Afterward, fried and tapped out, we'd turn on the TV and I'd eat a bowl of cereal with ice cream in it (don't hate, it's delicious). I'd stay up till my eyes burned just for the gift of a few moments of peace. Then we'd go to bed to do the whole thing over again, along with a billion loads of laundry just for fun.

In so many ways, I felt happy. I'd always wanted a family of my own, and even though I was exhausted, I felt fulfilled. Having a home, Graham, and my kids made me feel like I wasn't floating anymore. I belonged somewhere, and that was a giant relief.

But it did get lonely. Really lonely.

One night I was in the living room, lying on the blue-green

carpet remnant that Graham's aunt had given us. Graham was on the couch, and we were watching *The Biggest Loser.* I couldn't ignore the loneliness anymore. I'd been pushing it away, but now it seemed to physically walk into the room and sit down next to me. I turned off the TV and started sobbing. I wanted a close community so badly. I wanted people in my life who really knew me while I really knew them. I didn't want to just go through life detached and secluded in our own world of eating, sleeping, working, parenting, diaper changing, and TV watching. I wanted to do life with people. Graham looked up at me from where he was lying on the couch, caught off guard and possibly a little scared by this sudden outburst of emotion. "Uh, what just happened?"

"I'm just, um"—I tried to find the right words—"I'm so lonely for friendship." This caused more tears, and he sat up to face me.

"We have our families," he offered, referring to our siblings and parents who lived close by. "They're our friends."

"I know," I said, blowing my nose loudly, "and I'm so grateful that we do. I love them, they're amazing. They're just busy with their own lives and friends. They're also in different life stages than us. I guess I didn't realize it until right now, but I think I need more."

He thought for a minute. "I think I do, too." I was relieved to hear this; maybe I wasn't just being too needy.

As we sat in the dark living room, we began to flesh out what we felt was missing. We wanted the kind of friends who liked to stay up late and play games after our kids went to bed. We were parents, but we were still individuals, and we missed doing things with people that were just fun for the sake of fun. We wanted friends we could be ourselves around. Friends we could have real conversations with, joke with, and laugh with. Friends both of us meshed with (so neither of us would dread our time together). Friends who were flexible enough to meet up with on Sunday afternoon at the lake. Friends to just do life with.

We knew lots of people who could maybe be that for us, but they were in different seasons, were going different directions, or lived too far away to stop by on a random Tuesday afternoon. I was waiting for it to happen by accident, and it just wasn't happening.

"What should we do differently?" Graham asked.

"I don't know. We could try inviting people over, I guess?"

"Yeah, okay, what if we tried to do it once a week?"

"What if we chose a certain evening every week, like Friday, to keep it simple?"

We shared a look, one that said, *Yes, this will be good for us, but also, are we sure we want to commit to this out loud, in case it feels like a bad idea in the morning?*

"Sounds good," he said. We were doing it.

As much as I felt hope that night, I also felt terrified. While I knew I wanted a change, there was a part of me that liked spending all my nights in ratty sweatpants without a bra, binge-watching a mindless show. It was boring, but it was also safe and easy with zero chance of rejection. What if we invited these people over and they looked under our couch cushions and saw all the Cheerios and quarters in there and thought we were gross (and kind of wasteful, because there's like $5 worth in there)? Worse yet, what if we couldn't think of a single thing to say all night and they were like, "Wow, these are the most boring people we've ever met"?

At church that Sunday, we surveyed the people in the chairs in front of us, whispering back and forth about who to invite. We finally landed on a couple we'd met a few times.

"Let's do it," Graham said, like we'd just committed to bungee jumping.

I still get this way when I walk up to someone and invite them over. It feels like everything is out there on the table under the fluorescent light of a doctor's office, and you're about to find out if you do or don't have what it takes as a human. Am I good at humaning or bad at humaning? My whole life, I'd been basically avoiding finding out the answer to that question. In high school, a boy liked me, and I liked him back. He asked if he could call me, and I told him yes, then I left my house when I knew he was going to call so my mom could honestly tell him I was gone. I literally went on a five-mile run just to avoid that phone call. That same year, some girls who seemed fun and secure invited me to sit with them at lunch; I assumed they didn't mean it and sat by myself instead.

Those early months of getting out of my comfort zone and risking rejection were painful sometimes. No amount of head knowledge could convince my heart that I wasn't putting myself in imminent danger. The big change didn't happen because we suddenly weren't afraid. It came because we chose to ignore the fear and do it anyway.

It usually went something like this:

ME: Hey, I was just wondering if you guys would like to come over for dinner Friday?

MEANWHILE, INNER ME: What if they notice I haven't washed my hair since Tuesday? Is that gross? Am I gross? Oh no, is that egg on my pants? What if I seem desperate? I kind of am desperate, though . . . how does a desperate person seem not desperate? What if they really don't want to and then they have to think of excuses and it's really awkward and they . . .

THEM: We'd love to!

ME: Awesome! Can I get your number? I'll text you more details!

ALSO ME: What if they said yes out of pity? What if I can't think of one single thing to say all night long? What if they come over and it's so horrible they remember it forever as that one terrible night they went to that one family's house? What if we're weird and we don't even know it? *Oh my Gawd, what if our house has a smell and we don't smell it?*

THEM: Here you go! Let me know what I can bring.

ME: Sounds good!

Every Friday we'd frantically clean and cook. I'd agonize over the fact I was not the same girl as the one who'd invited these people. That girl was bold and full of reckless dreams. This girl worried about giving her guests food poisoning and was perfectly happy binge-watching *Suits* instead. She wasn't even sure she liked people very much. Kind of like when I signed up for a local CSA box because I was definitely going to cook more vegetables, and then the kale rotted in the crisper because real me thinks kale tastes like broken dreams. Graham and I would rush back and forth past each other, cleaning and cooking and silently trying to think of good excuses to cancel. Were we getting sick? Did the kids have a fever? Why on earth were we wishing someone had a fever? What was wrong with us?

And then the people would come, and it would be okay. We ate food, we talked, we survived. Sometimes it was great; sometimes we had moments of panic navigating awkward silences and burnt chicken. Every single time our guests went home, though, I felt a little bit freer and a little bit lighter. I felt infused with life, as if each and every connection had been cold water to my dehydrated soul. Even when we talked all night about their passion for NASCAR and cross-stitching, I felt oddly fulfilled.

With time, I felt more and more secure making asks. I found that people were not put out by my invitations the way I'd expected them to be. Instead, they were grateful. They told me how they had been lonely, too, and just hadn't known where to start in pursuing friends. Some even told me they'd wanted to get to know me but were intimidated by the idea of making the first move. They worried that their house was too small to host a big dinner, and what would they even cook?

There was rejection, too. Some people were indirect with their answers. "Oh yeah, we'll see what the week is like . . ." Others kept canceling when we tried to get together. One person in particular gave voice to my worst fears and unknowingly joked that I was boring. But to my great surprise, I lived, and I'm okay. I'm more than okay: I'm better for it.

I'm much stronger than I thought—and, my friend, so are you.

My value is no longer dependent on someone else's acceptance or rejection of me. It hurts when you put yourself out there and the answer is no, but I know my worth and I know my value, and that's something I had to go out and get on my own, one terrifying step at a time. That's what we don't realize when we're holed up in our comfort zones. The way we get stronger isn't by playing it safe; it's by stepping out.

We're just humans humaning. Every single time. No matter what fear you have, no matter what's holding you back, I can tell you it's universal at its core. Sure, some people seem to be born without the fear bone at all. They take charge of every situation and glide around parties like they're Beyoncé—but I call BS. All of us on some level are afraid of the exact same things; we just handle it differently. I have a friend who seems like the most secure person in the entire world, but if you ask her, she will tell you that she's often terrified, she just masks it by projecting security. If she hadn't told me that from her own lips, I wouldn't have believed it.

For me it's the most empowering thing in the world to know I'm not the only one. If I'd known that the people I was too scared to talk to were also scared, it would have dissolved my own insecurity in an instant.

If I never stepped out, I wouldn't have some of my most treasured friendships today. That's just a fact. Tonight Aubree and Benji are coming over for one of our let's-just-combine-our-fridges dinners and it's as simple as texting, *Hey, I have chicken, arugula, and tequila, what do you have?* and her responding, *Ice cream and blueberries, lol, should be good.*

It's been over a decade since we had them over for the first time. They've gotten married and have four kids now. We've added two to our own tribe. We've gone through countless highs and lows together, and we're family now. Like, real family. Her younger kids have no idea that I'm not their real aunt.

When I think of the cost versus the reward, it's incomparable. If I'd known that behind that door of fear would be these deep and precious friendships, I would never have questioned it for a second.

The first year of inviting people to our home was all about planting new seeds. As with a garden, we didn't see a lot of fruit immediately. It can take time, but every awkward introduction ("Hey, I'm Jess") will bring you closer. Every invitation will be like turning on the light in your room and looking under your bed to find a granola bar wrapper, a couple of forks, and zero monsters.

STEP SIX: Ignore the Fear and Get Going

How scared are you of rejection on a scale of 1 through 10?

1: I'm not, that's not really my deal.

5: I'm scared, but it doesn't stop me from putting myself out there.

10: I would rather give myself a tattoo blindfolded than risk rejection.

If you're a 1, awesome. You've either done the work or you were just born that way.

If you're the one who usually does the pursuing and initiating, it can be easy to assume that other people are selfish or disinterested. Don't forget to factor in that they may just be scared. You might be so good at being the pursuer that others feel they could never measure up. They may be so busy thinking they're not good enough that it hasn't occurred to them that anyone would want their pursuit.

If you're a 5, go you.

Doing it scared is a fantastic way to be. Keep refusing to allow your fear to control you—and if you're comfortable doing this, start to share your eternal battle with other people. It might be just the encouragement someone else needs to step out of their own comfort zone. Challenge yourself. Is there any area you're still holding back in? Maybe without even realizing it? If so, you got this.

If you're a 10, fantastic. I've been right exactly in your shoes. Take a moment to evaluate what your fear of rejection is holding you back from. I can't take a single step for you—no one can. But I can tell you that freedom is on the other side. Yes, the bubble is nice and safe, but it's also inhibiting you from connection. Write one thing down that is outside your comfort zone that you're going to do this week. Maybe it's a dinner invite or asking someone to coffee. Maybe it's simply striking up a conversation with someone new at your kid's soccer game.

Wherever you're at, remember you're not alone. You can do this. Also, pro tip: Most people love box brownies, and they're the easiest, cheapest things in the world.

LIE #7: My Job Is to Keep People Happy and Make Sure They Like Me

3/15/1990 (five years old)

Dear Diary,

Two of my friends came over to play. They kept fighting over who got to be the bride in our game and who had to be the groom, so I just said I'd be the preacher and I spent all day marrying them over and over. Sometimes I had to be the groom.

It was not fun at all, but at least they stopped fighting. Kind of. They kept pulling me over to the corner and asking me if I was *their* best friend only, so I said yes to both of them. That was awkward.

I think I'm going to make my brother marry me later so I get to be the bride for once.

Love,

Jess

The goal is to make everyone happy, right?
Read also:

Meet everyone's expectations.
Be the good guy.
Never make anyone uncomfortable.

Accommodate everyone's needs.
Be all things to all people.

Now excuse me while I go hide in my closet and have an anxiety attack.

I consider myself to be a pretty strong person. I live under the delusion that should I be attacked in an alleyway, I would win. I'm like a Yorkshire terrier that believes she's a pit bull. (Aubree does not share this faith in my abilities and makes me run with her to the car.) I'm the kind of girl who loads her arms with twenty-three grocery bags rather than asking for help, so it's embarrassing to admit how much I struggle with other people's opinions of me. I know better; it's just a lot of work to *do* better.

I worked at a bakery and sandwich shop once. I've loved almost every job I've ever had, but this was the one I dreaded walking into. The space was cold and sterile, like a hospital cafeteria. The lights were high and bright, and the temperature was never turned up past I-should-have-worn-thicker-socks degrees. The vibe just wasn't vibing, as my teenagers would say. Plus, I worked only once a week, so I never quite found my groove. I basically kept that job purely for the little pieces of pastry that would be left on the pan when I scraped off the cinnamon rolls to fill the display. I'm not sure if everyone else was eating those, but I was. Job: 2 out of 5 stars. Cinnamon rolls: 5 out of 5.

One day when things were slow, I asked if I could redraw the specials on the chalkboard up front. They said I could, so I climbed up on the counter and set to work. I love to draw, and decorating chalkboards is one of my favorite things. I was going to make this the most beautiful specials board that had ever existed. I erased the scrawled Reuben special from the day before and drew the first lines of my masterpiece.

Nowadays, I know about my ADHD, but then I didn't. As I

drew, the whole world disappeared. It was just me and the chalk. I didn't hear anything, and I didn't see anything. I carefully crafted each letter in calligraphy and doodled a cartoon sandwich giving a to-go cup a high five. It looked great and I was proud that I had found a way to contribute.

My trance was suddenly interrupted by the gravelly voice of my boss. *"What are you doing?"* he snapped, visibly angry. *"Stop messing around and get down here to help."* I felt verbally slapped.

During my trance, the bakery had gotten busy. There were lines at both of the registers. Two of my co-workers were frantically taking orders while the other one raced to box up baked goods. I hadn't noticed a thing. My body went tingly, and I felt like bursting into tears. I climbed down and jumped in to help, stumbling over an apology. I went into autopilot as I took orders, but everything in me wanted to run away and cry. There was something about his tone, something about the way he said it, that made me feel so small.

What I heard him say wasn't that I'd made a mistake and needed to pay more attention next time. I heard him say that I got it wrong because I was lazy, selfish, and inconsiderate as a person. I knew that I wasn't trying to leave my co-workers high and dry, but his tone made me question my motives. Maybe I was a bad employee. Maybe even a bad person. Even now, after years and years of learning that I'm not responsible for someone else's anger, it is a battle every time to get my head straight.

Hi, I'm Jess and I'm a people pleaser. I also dabble in codependency just for fun.

I really want you to like me and I really, really want you not to be mad at me. I also don't want you to feel anything icky when you're around me. Like, I don't want you to feel bad about yourself, either, so if you tell me that you're struggling with something that I don't struggle with, I will try really, really hard to struggle with it, too, so you don't feel alone. If you are having an insecure day, I will make it my personal mission to infuse you with confidence. If you are sad and I cannot seem to cheer you up, then I will try harder. I'm pretty good at putting myself in other people's shoes, even if I can't relate to what they're feeling personally.

Years ago, I had a friend who was passionate about nutrition and very careful about what she ate. I'm not going to say I'm careless, but I'm not above a McDonald's cheeseburger, and I definitely have a favorite order (and sauce) at Chick-fil-A. (Spicy chicken sandwich meal with extra pickles, a vanilla milkshake, and honey mustard, because I know you were wondering.) My friend could vent to me about how bothered she was that her sister-in-law fed her kids chicken nuggets, even though we both knew my kids ate chicken nuggets. Instead of taking offense or interjecting my opinions—like, "Hey, my kid ate a chicken nugget off the Suburban floor yesterday, and they seemed fine"— I was more like, "That's really frustrating that you don't feel like you're taken seriously by your sister-in-law." I did and do value that about our friendship.

Over many years of friendship, our differences grew more and more. They became about more important things like core values and worldview. I still appreciated our ability to support each other despite our differences, but there was one thing she was venting about a lot that I really didn't agree with, something that had a much bigger impact than either of our opinions on fast food. For a long time, I continued to do what I always do: I listened with empathy. But I began to feel like I was betraying my own convictions by not telling her the truth about what I thought. I still wanted to be a safe place for her, but I needed to be honest.

So I was. I told her that I didn't agree. I didn't need her to see it my way, I just needed her to know where I stood. I tried my best to wrap it up in bows and ribbons and encouragement so that it wouldn't upset her or hurt her . . . and it went as poorly as it possibly could go. In her story, I became someone who didn't respect her, and our connection dissolved after that.

That was hard for me to swallow. I'd worked to be supportive for so long, I thought I'd earned the right to challenge her on this thing that mattered to me. Instead, I realized I'd built an expectation that I would go with her flow.

In her defense, I completely set her up. I waited too long. I hadn't wanted to hurt her feelings, I hadn't wanted to make her feel alienated, and, selfishly, I simply hadn't wanted her to be mad at me, so I went along with things that didn't feel right for me. I buried my own need to be heard for a long time. It was unfair to her and to me.

Now I see that I was taking the easy way out. Being nice isn't always nice. Not hurting someone's feelings isn't always the kind thing. Keeping the peace isn't always the most peaceful in the long run.

It is my default factory setting to prioritize other people's needs over my own, and the tragic part is that it happens most with people I love or respect. I tell myself, *They have bigger needs than me; I can take it,* but that's a cop-out. The truth is I'm just scared. I'm scared to have needs. I'm scared of rocking the boat. I'm scared of saying no. I'm scared of being perceived as difficult or sensitive. I'm scared I won't be able to handle it if they're angry with me—or, worse, reject me.

I wrestled with that broken relationship for a long time. I went over it again and again in my mind. I talked to my therapist about it nearly every time I went to see her. "I'm just still struggling because there is no peace; it feels like this file I can't put away. I want to do more to fix it, but everything I do seems to make it worse." I wanted to put the thing to rest, but it was just so hard.

I thought about how I could have done it differently, but I know now that thing I had to do was a hard thing. "There wasn't another way," my therapist said. "You had to do what you knew was right for you." She didn't say it in a way that made the other woman a villain; it just was what it was. Her right and my right were not aligned.

How could something be right for me and seemingly so wrong for someone else?

I don't know. I'm not in charge of that part. They can be angry, and I can be doing the right thing for me. Both things can be true.

As humans, we really, really want there to be black-and-white answers, a hero and a villain. I want to be able to walk away from a situation and write in my diary: *I was a sweetheart, and she was a big jerk, and that is why we can no longer be friends.* Then I want all my friends and family to affirm this is true: "Yeah, she's definitely the problem and you are precious and wonderful, and you handled everything with such wisdom and grace."

"She had to do what was best for her, and I had to do what was best for me" feels a lot harder to swallow, and I don't love it; it's uncomfortable. It makes the work of honoring myself more difficult, but it gets at a deeper truth: I need to validate my own feelings and needs *even when* the other person isn't bad or wrong.

Being the bad guy in someone's story does not make you a bad guy.

Someone being angry with you doesn't mean you're wrong.

The goal isn't to make people happy.

It also isn't your job to keep people happy.

You'd think that following along and not rocking the boat would lead to greater connection, but I find the opposite is true. If you have to hide parts of yourself to keep the peace, if you have to minimize your needs to make things work, if you have to play a specific role to stay friends, then while you might save the face of your friendship, it will be shallow. It won't give you the depth you desire. Faking it till you make it isn't a thing when it comes to friendship. If we don't authentically show up in our relationships, true belonging can't happen.

When I don't show up honestly in a friendship, I start to pull away, sometimes without even realizing it. I feel exhausted whenever I spend time with them. I start to go into autopilot, going through the motions of friendship, unwilling to admit my heart isn't there anymore. Part of the problem is that I'm lying to the other person, but a bigger issue is that I'm lying to myself.

I don't know who needs to hear this, but stop acting like you're not a human with needs and preferences. It might feel like the better option, but it's not.

They might not know something is missing, but you will.

People pleasing doesn't affect just my friendships; it shows up in other areas, too, like parenting. I particularly dread the times when I have to give out tough love. Trust me, I do not get good feedback from my kids when I give them chores or tell them it's time to get up in the morning. If I want to keep my peace, I cannot gauge my actions by their level of happiness with me.

One of my kids wakes up kicking and screaming. He reminds me of Jim Carrey in *Bruce Almighty* when his alarm goes off in the morning, writhing and thrashing like the sunlight is assaulting him personally. Another one thinks washing the dishes is the exact same thing as being asked to walk across hot coals and is convinced that I basically enjoy torturing people. Another one thinks eating is annoying. All of them spend a lot of time not being happy with me. As a feely, people-pleasing person, I find this exhausting. Occasionally after a battle, I'll go get in my bed and pull the covers over my head or stick my face in the freezer and shovel some cookie dough ice cream into my face. *You are a Viking,* I tell myself. *You can do this. Just because they don't like you right now doesn't mean you're doing it wrong. It might mean you're doing it right.*

It doesn't always make me feel better, but I know it's true, and I persist.

I'd rather do all the chores myself than deal with the melt-downs, to be honest. Sometimes that's exactly what I do. *But* I force myself to have needs and not to do it all, because my job isn't their temporary happiness, it's teaching them how to be well-adjusted humans. It's showing them that even though the world seems like it's ending right here right now as they survey all the dog poop in the backyard, it's not. It's teaching them to find their inner resilience, even when there are twenty turds in the yard for them to pick up and now it's raining.

Those are my children. I actually am in charge of them. I'm not in charge of another single soul on this planet. If it's not my job to make my kids happy constantly, it sure as heck isn't to make anyone else happy.

I'm not advocating that we plow over people's hearts or stop taking responsibility for our actions. There have been many times when someone has gotten angry with me because I screwed up. In those cases, I'm still not in charge of their anger, but I am in charge of cleaning up my mess with them. I am in charge of taking responsibility for the ways I let them down or hurt them and apologizing.

I ended up apologizing to my friend from that earlier scenario, because she told me that the way I shared my convictions left her feeling disrespected. I had been so scared to have that conversation, and I knew I hadn't communicated well. I told her I understood why my delivery made her feel that way and I was really sorry. I clarified things that had left her confused. I apologized for not talking to her about it sooner. I told her how sorry I was that I hurt her. But after that, I had to let it go. It was out of my hands and in hers. She didn't have to forgive me. She didn't have to be happy with me. Only she knows what is right for her.

Don't play the groom every time (unless you want to be the groom!). Don't minimize your needs in order to accommodate someone else. Don't shame yourself because of someone else's anger issue. It's hard work, but it's good work.

It took me a full year to find peace over that falling-out with my friend. I still wrestle with it, but only occasionally. It's in my rearview mirror now, and I'm proud of myself for having the hard conversation. I'm proud of myself for sitting in the uncomfortable reality of unresolved conflict. I'm proud of myself for not backpedaling, even when I wanted to.

If I could go back in time and talk to my boss at the bakery, I would tell him:

Hey, Stan (not his name, but it should be, he looked like a Stan),

You seemed stressed, I'm sorry. I'm sure it's hard to believe, but I didn't realize how busy it had gotten, and that's my fault. I will work on being more aware of my surroundings, because that's probably really annoying for a lot of people. Chalkboard art doesn't seem like a high priority to you, and I get that. Your cinnamon rolls are killer, your sandwiches are fine, you're a straightforward guy, and you don't need fancy signs to get your point across. That said, I'm working three jobs right now, and I'm not even sure why I'm here. I like your cream cheese frosting a lot, but I don't really like anything else about this place. It's cold. Your lighting choices are bad. You're pretty rude. You don't pay me very well. I don't even like cold sandwiches. You don't serve pickles and that stinks. Anyway. That's just a small sampling of some things I've been thinking about lately.

Chalkboard art isn't for you, I respect that. This job isn't for me, I hope you can understand. If not, might I suggest a cinnamon roll, it's very comforting.

Peace out, Stan.

STEP SEVEN: Stop Trying to Keep People Happy

Ask yourself:

Am I showing up in my life as a person with needs, wants, and desires?

In what areas am I listening to my own heart?

Where am I undermining my own voice to keep the peace?

What is one need it's time to get real about?

A friend of mine has been working on having boundaries with someone who didn't know how to honor her needs. She is someone who naturally bends over backward for the people she loves, so this was very challenging for her, particularly when the person became upset with her. My friend immediately felt confused. Was she doing the right thing? They were so mad, it seemed like she wasn't. She told me that her counselor said something that changed her perspective.

He said: "Anytime you're confused, it's because you're taking on someone else's feelings. Because your feelings aren't confusing."

Stop trying to consider how others might react to your

needs, or how it might inconvenience them. It's making it confusing, and your feelings shouldn't be confusing. They might be hard to access if you've been ignoring them for a long time, and you might have to be patient with yourself as you work to unbury them, but they're not confusing, because they're yours. Once you turn down the other noise in your head, you'll be able to find them.

LIE #8: Neighbors Are Weird

Dear Diary,

Today I met my neighbor.

I told her I have four kids.

She said that was fine, "as long as they're quiet."

I'm not sure she's met kids before.

So now I'm looking for a place to move, or some kind of cloaking device for my children.

Any ideas?

Love,

Jess

Neighbors can be a weird concept when you grew up in the woods—or in my husband's case, on a farm. I might know my neighbors or not know them, but they're some of the only people who've seen me without a bra, frantically pulling my garbage cans to the curb. "Hey, George, I don't know where you grew up or what your last name is, but I'm going to stand here with my arms crossed in front of my chest chatting about the weather, and later I might invite you inside my house to feed my cat while I go out of town."

When we think about loneliness and our desire to live a connected life, we usually focus on finding our next BFF instead of looking for the connections in our community that are literally all around us. Casual acquaintances aren't the same thing as a friend who knows all your secrets and helps herself to a LaCroix from your fridge, but they do provide a sense of belonging and roots that makes you feel grounded. I think we know this, deep down. It's why TV shows with towns like Stars Hollow or Virgin River suck us in. Something in us longs for a little community where everyone knows everyone.

Today there are a million things that keep us from making those connections: busyness, Instacart and grocery pickup, working from home, Amazon Prime—I could go on. I love all of those conveniences. Grocery pickup is saving my life right now, and the gift of just clicking a button to order something oddly specific like a Ted Lasso Christmas sweater rather than scouring the shelves in five different stores is . . . like, an actual miracle. But they've also created a scenario where for most of us, neighborly connections don't happen as organically as they once did. I wonder if that's partly why so many of us feel lonely and isolated.

I didn't have a Taylor Doose with an ice cream shop or a mayor like Hope McCrea, but I did get the privilege of being a part of two small towns with their own larger-than-life characters. The town my family moved to in Montana was small, with just five hundred people. It was small enough that one time when I forgot to pay for gas on my way to snowboard, the owner of the gas station called my mom, then he called me. "Hey honey, it's Mike," he said. "You forgot to pay for your gas. Just come back when you're done on the mountain, no rush." The town still feels small enough that when I went back to visit a few years ago, my trunk popped open on the highway, and someone called my best friend (who was in California) to ask her to call me and tell me. Small enough that when I went grocery shopping and forgot my wallet, the cashier insisted that I bring the food home and come back with my debit card, because otherwise the ice cream would melt. Small enough that when Graham had a bad fall roofing and broke his wrist, we knew the EMTs from down the street, and the doctor who fixed him up was the same one who'd helped him after a fall when he was five years old.

Not everyone lives in a small town where everyone knows everyone and the owner of the movie store also owns the pizza shop and takes care of the town's fireworks (and also will tow you out of a ditch). I don't either, anymore. Some people would say I do, but there are at least two dozen streetlights here, so not by my standards. There are still ways to find connection in your community, though, even if you feel lost in a sea of faces. Connection and belonging can come from the places you least expect if you open your heart and pay attention.

It doesn't have to be the people who live on your actual street, especially if your neighbor hates children (see above diary entry), but it can be. My friend's neighborhood has a nightly happy-hour walk where the moms pull out their strollers and Stanley mugs filled with wine and manage the witching hour together. I love that.

My go-to move is choosing a coffee shop, preferably near my house, where I can become a regular. Yes, I can make coffee at home, but I consider it a way to get out at least three times a week and connect with my community. No matter where I've lived or where I've gone, coffee shops always have a small-town vibe. If you order the same thing every time, the baristas will start to remember. They'll probably learn your name and you'll learn theirs, too. You can be intentional about asking questions and you'll start to get to know them. Another key is to tip well. It's not paying them to be your friend; it's showing them that you value them.

We like to do that with a local brewery or restaurant, too. (Again, tip well!) Become a regular and you'll get to know people

Luke's-Diner-style, even if you're in a busy city. For me half of it is the food and vibe (or coffee and vibe), and the other half is the people there (whether they're employees or regular patrons). Are they stuffy and uptight, or are they warm and welcoming? Are they friendly and open or focused and busy? I'm not looking for best-friend material, but it should be noted that I have experienced good friendships that started with long chats at the coffee drive-up window or by becoming regulars at a breakfast spot.

The options are endless. Join a church or a book club. Get to know the other parents when your kids are in sports. Volunteer at your kid's school or join a team-style gym. Get creative. Maybe your coffee shop is a dog park or a grocery store. You can become a regular anywhere. Maybe it will lead to close friendship, or maybe it will just lead to feeling like you're a part of things, like people know you. Both forms of connection are worth it.

There were two bars on the river: One in the tiny community where my family lived, and one in the tiny community I was bused to. The first was in the double-wide along with my dad's office and a small grocery. The other one used to have a storefront, but the building burned down. It became a picnic table under a tree, and they called it the beer tree.

If you went to the beer tree, you would usually find the same crew there, catching up after work and telling stories. One of the regulars was iconic in our community. He looked large and intimidating, towering over the other men and women, but he was friendly. The stories about him were almost like fables—usually involving a trip to the beer tree first. I'd overhear my friends' parents telling stories: "Remember the time he drove straight off the road and we thought he was dead, but he was just spinning brodies in his Bronco on the riverbank?" If he showed you his belly, people said, it was covered in scars from knife wounds and bullet holes. When I asked why he had those scars, I was just told he had been in a lot of fights. He seemed nice to me, but I also figured you didn't want to cross him.

One night my dad had switched off the generator and we had all gone to bed by candlelight when tires screeched on the road above us. We heard slamming doors and yelling. Keep in mind that we were miles from the nearest house and people rarely drove by, especially at night. When no one within fifty miles is playing a radio or watching a TV, it is a powerful kind of quiet. The yelling caused shock waves to run down my spine and goose bumps to cover my arms. My parents blew out all the candles except for one and told us to keep our voices down. The night was deep black with only a sliver of a moon. I was terrified. I could hear a man screaming at a woman, "You better come back!"

My dad told my sixteen-year-old cousin, who was visiting for the weekend, to follow him outside and watch the door while he went up to check out the situation. My cousin tensed—he lived in urban Los Angeles and didn't seem confident about the plan. I thought for a minute about the lack of streetlights and emergency response, and I didn't blame him. I really didn't want Dad to go, and I don't think my mom did, either. I could hear her whispering to him in hushed tones when suddenly, we heard the scratching of someone's fingernails on the door. I jumped out of my skin.

A woman's voice came through the window. "Please," she called quietly, "please let me in." Followed by more scratching. They opened the door gently, to keep it from creaking, and guided her in. The voices on the road got louder and angrier once they realized the woman was gone. It was a miracle she'd even found our house in the pitch black. Without a generator or any kind of light, you couldn't see the place from the road.

I remember my mom bringing her to the kitchen, and my dad

telling me to take my brother to my room before he nodded at my cousin and they headed out the door.

In my room, my brother and I lay face down on the floor—I guess so I could worry better. "You scared?" my brother asked.

"No," I said.

"Me neither," he answered.

It seemed like hours before my dad's voice reemerged in the living room. He was telling my mom that he was going to start the generator. When the lights came on we ventured back out and saw a frail blond woman shivering in my great-grandmother's rocker. I'd never been around anyone that high before. My drunk neighbor took care of me after school once, but she just kept telling me the same story about how her dog had been limping since Tuesday and she didn't know why, over and over again. This was different. The woman from the road was sitting, shaking, covered in a blanket. Then she cried out suddenly, tears running down her face. I jumped—then, right after that outburst, she sneezed a high-pitched, whistling sneeze and shouted, "*I sneeze like a cat!*" before she started laughing hysterically. I tried not to stare, but it was hard. She giggled to herself, then looked over at me. "I sneeze like a cat." I didn't say anything, just stared at her blankly, but it didn't matter. She was hysterically laughing again.

"Jessica," my mom said, "time for bed."

The next morning, the woman was in my kitchen drinking tea. She seemed calm and normal, like someone who might be a substitute teacher at my school, or a friend's aunt that came to town. She was soft-spoken, not like the night before. I doubted she remembered sneezing like a cat, but I sure was going to remember it for the rest of my life. Later, after my dad had driven her where she needed to go, I heard the rest of the story.

My dad had gone up to meet the men on the road. It turned

out that we did know them, or at least knew who they were. One was the big man from the beer tree. The other was a man known for being dangerous and unpredictable.

My dad saw the dangerous one first. He looked ready to fight my dad and demanded to see his girlfriend.

"I don't think tonight," my dad said calmly. "I just think she needs to rest tonight."

"I want to see her!" he snarled. "Where is she?"

Right then, the big man appeared around the other side of the truck, giant and towering, his face apprehensive. When he saw my dad, his shoulders relaxed, and his tense expression shifted into a wide smile.

"Oh hey!" he said, suddenly delighted. "It's the preacher! Hey, Preacher!

"Be nice!" he added, turning to his friend. "This is the preacher!"

Years earlier, my dad had gone regularly to pray with one of the big man's close family members when she was very ill. The man was quiet; he'd stood stoically in the room while my dad was there, and they never talked. One of her dying requests was for my dad to share at her memorial. He did, high in the mountains at the family's burial grounds. He'd ridden with the family quietly up a long dirt road in the back of a pickup truck, and they solemnly honored her life together. My dad wasn't sure how the man felt about him being there, and he'd felt acutely like an outsider. Again, they never spoke.

Now the same man reached out his giant hand and put it on my dad's shoulder. "You sure touched my life, Preacher, somethin' special."

His friend held a knife. "Where is she?" he demanded.

"She's safe with my wife," said my dad.

"We're not going anywhere," growled the dangerous man.

"Naw," the big man said. "We're going to go. You leave him alone. What are you thinking?"

The two of them left that night, and no harm came to anyone.

I remember hearing the rest of that story and feeling grateful we were safe, but mostly feeling proud that the larger-than-life man from the beer tree was friends with my dad. I'm not saying you should befriend people in your community so they can save you from scary men with knives, but I am telling you that getting involved and showing up matters. To be a part of stuff, you have to show up, like my dad did, riding far into the mountains because he'd been asked to.

It can seem trivial and unnecessary to walk into a coffee shop, and OMG is it easier to order groceries than to physically go into a store, but there's something valuable about doing life with your neighbors (whether they live right by you or not).

There's something special about simply being known and knowing people in your town. It might not happen organically, but it can happen with some intentionality.

Something else I learned during that time on the river is the value of friendship with people who think differently, live differently, and believe differently. I was raised Christian, but most of my friends were not Christians. I believed in Jesus while they believed in other spirits or nothing at all, and it taught me respect for other worldviews.

When we moved, I made friends with some kids who were also Christians. I liked them as friends, but one thing threw me off. They hung out only with Christians, and when they talked about people we knew who were not Christians, they had a certain tone. The tone said those people were not the same as them, that they were "bad," or scary, or unsafe. If we keep our worlds small and surround ourselves only with people who think just like us, we can become judgmental and ignorant, thinking we have a monopoly on truth. Connecting in our communities with people who have different faiths, different worldviews, different backgrounds, different ethnicities, and different lifestyles is healthy and wholesome. It's also a great way to keep from becoming a jerk.

I'll end this chapter with a story that touched my heart.

A couple of years ago we were renting out our camper, and we went to deliver it to a house across town. Our city has minimal rentals available, and people sometimes rented our camper to serve as a guesthouse, or as a living space while they did renovations. I instantly wanted to adopt the woman who was renting it this time as my aunt. She was warm and friendly, her gray hair pulled back into a clip, a holiday apron tied around her waist. She brought us homemade peanut brittle as we set everything up. She was using the camper for her son who was coming to town with his family for Christmas, and she couldn't wait.

Her home was beautiful, with vines draped idyllically over the dormers. We commented on how lovely it was. "You know, we used to live in that house," she said, pointing to one across the street. She smiled with nostalgia. "There used to be an elderly woman who lived in this house. She seemed like she was always on her own, so we decided to include her in things. We started bringing her cookies, and pretty soon she was joining us for family meals and on the holidays. I'd send my kids over to mow her lawn and do projects for her. We became family."

She teared up at this part and cleared her throat. "About ten years ago she passed away, and . . . she left us her house." She wiped her eyes. "I couldn't believe it, we were so shocked, we never in a million years could have seen that coming. We enjoyed being around her so much, I just didn't think it was any great thing for us to do. We were just being neighbors."

The most beautiful connections can come from places you

least expect them. I could be wrong, but I'd be willing to bet that the gift that family gave her was greater even than the value of that house.

STEP EIGHT: Weird (aka Different) Is Good, and Communities Are Full of Opportunities for Connection

Your goal might be to find your version of Sookie and Lorelai, but don't forget about Michel, Miss Patty, Babette, and Kirk. All those other relationships make life full, too. (As in, you're not just looking for main characters here; you're looking for side characters and even cast extras.)

If you don't feel connected in your community, think of one place you can start investing in regularly, even if it's by buying your favorite latte more often than you usually do, and from the same spot. Work to learn people's names and remember details about their lives. It will mean more to them than you know, and could even open avenues for deeper connection.

Neighbors are a gift. Living in a community keeps us grounded. Now go out and find your Stars Hollow.

LIE #9: Asking for Help Is a Terrible Idea, Because Then Everyone Is Going to Know I Need Help

5/10/2009

Dear Diary,

Today I went to the grocery store with the boys.

Scout (who is three months old) woke up and started screaming in his car seat. Malachi (who is two) wouldn't sit down. He kept saying something repeatedly, and I was like, "Yep, uh-huh," because I couldn't understand him.

I kept giving Scout his paci in the checkout line so I could get outside and nurse in the car.

Right as I was about to put the milk on the conveyor belt, I noticed a horrific smell wafting from that area. Then I saw that the mustard had somehow exploded on everything in the cart.

Then I realized it wasn't mustard, and the thing Malachi was trying to say was "I poop."

Someone asked me if I needed help, and I said no, thank you.

Love,

Jess

GOD: How are you doing?

ME: Horrible. I'm actually drowning in stuff I have to do, and I'm about to lose my mind. Please give me more strength.

GOD: Did you ask for help from someone?

ME: No, I just want to do it, so if you could make this cold and headache go away and also give me Superman powers and speed, that would be perfect.

GOD: Didn't Lisa already offer to help?

ME: I just don't think you're hearing me. I don't need help like that, I need you to just make me more efficient and less congested.

GOD: You should see what Lisa is up to.

glance at the clock. It's five o'clock and I have one hour until tonight's guests arrive, so I grab throw pillows and start fluffing frantically. I am beating them back to life like I'm performing couch CPR. My daughter wanders through the living room unsuspectingly with her earbuds in, listening to music. "Oaklee, did you clean your room?" I ask wildly, still providing lifesaving services to a lumbar pillow from World Market.

"Huh?" she asks, taking out one earbud.

"Did you pick up the entryway like I asked?"

"Yeah," she says, calm and aloof.

It's like she doesn't even understand this crisis. I give one last smack to the pillow and glance at the entryway on my way to the kitchen. The shoes have been shoved to the side in a large, stinky mountain. I feel like my head is going to launch off my neck, like a rocket on its way to Mars. I can't do it all, this is too much, but if I don't do it myself it won't be done right.

My son walks past me, and I see him headed for the couch, my life flashing before my eyes. I see the plop before it happens. He drops his backpack on the ground and falls back in slow motion onto my perfectly fluffed pillows.

"Noooooo," I gasp. He looks at me like I'm speaking Latin. I know I am ridiculous. I know this is ridiculous.

My phone pings. It's from tonight's guests: *Hey, at the store, can I bring something?*

No, you're good! I reply, adding three emojis to emphasize how excited and not at all overwhelmed I am, and hit SEND.

My son raises his eyebrows at me, and I raise mine back even higher and shake my head, like it's an eyebrow-raising contest and I am clearly winning. "Can you just, like, not sit down until people get here?" I say.

An hour later a candle is lit, music is playing, and I am smiling as I open the door like I'm Martha freaking Stewart and haven't stressed a day in my life.

"I can't believe you didn't want us to bring anything," says our guest. "Your house is beautiful, and it smells wonderful."

I think about all the random crap I just stuffed in my closet. "Oh, it was no big deal!" I smile. "So easy."

My son wanders in and says hello. "Hey, Mom," he asks, "am I allowed to sit down now?" He is trolling me, and he knows it.

Are you also help-resistant—some might even call it receiving-help-impaired? Do you enjoy taking on too much, not asking for help, not accepting help, and then getting super overwhelmed and stressed, taking it out on your loved ones, and being like, "I don't know what's wrong with me"? If you're not quite as much of a basket case as I am, do you at least say yes to things you definitely shouldn't say yes to sometimes? Say, "Naw, I got it," when someone offers to carry a bag for you (even when you clearly do not "got" it)?

Psychology Today suggests we don't ask for help because (a) We don't want to be a burden, (b) We don't want to be seen as vulnerable or weak, and (c) We make assumptions that people don't want to help.

All those things are true for me. I don't want to be a burden, and even more than that I don't want to feel like I am a burden. It's almost like the weight of wondering if I am a burden feels more stressful than just doing it on my own.

Asking for help does feel vulnerable. It feels scary to let someone know that I need help and even scarier that they might say no. I absolutely assume people don't want to be inconvenienced, and that leaves me scared about a and b all over again. Either they'll say yes even though they don't want to and I'll be a burden, or they'll say no because I'm too much and they don't want to be inconvenienced.

I think there is a part of me that's always trying to fill a secret savings account. I'm trying to give and give to the people I love, so that if I ever desperately need to make a withdrawal, the investment will be there. I want to give enough to feel certain that if I ever need help, people will show up for me. I want to create security that I won't ever be alone.

If I just straight up ask for help with little things, I might find out I'm not worth it, and that terrifies me. I might find out I'm alone, and that right there is my biggest fear of all.

Years ago, Aubree stepped in and changed my perspective entirely. I was in the middle of the worst season of anxiety I've ever had. Years of pregnancy, breastfeeding, and being in a constant state of overwhelm finally took their toll. For an entire month, I couldn't leave the house without having a panic attack. It was unfamiliar territory; I had never felt so unglued. I'd wake up in the morning with the weight of a fifty-gallon drum sitting on my chest, feelings of fear and dread consuming my every waking thought. When I tried taking the kids out to the playground or the beach to do normal things, I'd start to get waves of panic that I couldn't deflect, finally melting down into tears wherever I was at.

I still didn't know how to ask for help, but I didn't have to. Aubree had struggled with anxiety all her life, and even though I was terrified of what was going on, she wasn't. She tells me to this day that she had no idea she was doing anything important, but what she did changed my life. Every single day she would stop by my house to check on me. We would sit on the back porch. I'd be paralyzed and lifeless, trapped in my own head with no idea how to escape. She would ask me, "What are you afraid of today?"

I would tell her all the panicked thoughts racing through my head, and she would nod calmly, and then she would look into my eyes and say, "That thing you're scared of? It's just anxiety. It's not going to happen, and you don't have anything to worry about." It was like being lost and alone in the dark when suddenly a hand reaches out to grab yours. *I've got you; this is the way.* Every time she came over, I would weep and weep. Every time she left, I'd feel grounded again (precariously, but still). The next morning I'd wake up exactly the same way, with the fifty-gallon drum on my chest, but she did not give up on me. She just kept showing up.

It's easy to forget that the people who love us genuinely want to help. When they ask, "What can I bring?" it's because they actually want to contribute. When they ask, "What can I do?" it's because they really do want to help. When we say "no" or "I've got it," we're not only cheating ourselves, we're also cheating them out of an opportunity to be a part of something.

When a friend asked me to be there when her daughter was born, it was the best gift. When another friend suffered a miscarriage and I sat with her on the bathroom floor crying and grieving, it was awful, and it was a sacred invitation. When I've gotten to stand alongside my friends on their wedding days, it's been a precious thing. When I've sat with my friends at the funerals of their loved ones, there's nowhere I'd want to be but right there in that moment with them holding their hands and their hearts. It is an honor to be there. One of life's greatest honors. It's being human together, irreparably human.

My mother-in-law is the queen of pulling you into whatever it is she's doing. If you walk into her kitchen, she will embrace you, she will ask you about your life and offer you a drink, and then she will hand you a potato peeler. Some of my favorite times at her house are spent sitting at her big red table chopping veggies and talking. There is something about the busyness and the camaraderie of it that makes you feel like you belong.

I want nothing more than to be that kind of host, but I'm a chaotic force in the kitchen, using my ADHD hyperfocus to complete five dishes at once (and all on high heat). When people ask what they can do, I'm like a deer in the headlights. "Um, I don't know?" I never know what I need, and I also don't know where the knife or cutting board is. I struggle with pulling people in the way she does, but I've learned to be like her in other ways. I say yes when my friends ask if they can bring a dish (even though I "could" make that salad). They bring their makings over and set to work chopping while I try not to burn things on the stove. One of my friends, Lindsay, doesn't even ask anymore, she just brings over a favorite bottle of wine and pours us each a glass while I chop. There's nothing like sweating over a hot pan and having a friend hand you a cold glass of your favorite white.

We are absolutely bombarded with messages that we need to do it all. Be a mom, but be a career woman, too, and make sure you give 100 percent in both places. Make your kids your world, but don't make your world about your kids. Be good at keeping house, but also you'd better make time for "self-care," whatever that means. Don't spend too much money on groceries, but buy organic and healthy food. Make sure your kids eat, but not that junk, but also don't force them to eat things they don't want to eat. Make sure your kids aren't jerks, but also don't set any limits and let them lead. Follow your dreams, but don't rock the boat. Exercise, but don't be obsessed with it, because that's annoying.

Drink more water, but don't take too many pee breaks; no one wants to wait for you. Be calm and poised no matter what is happening around you, but for God's sake don't let anything bad happen to anyone you love because is anyone really paying as much attention as you are?

When everything in us believes we should be doing it all, "I need help" is one of the bravest things we can say.

"I can't" is a powerful admission.

"I don't know how" isn't weakness. It is strength.

Not carrying sixteen grocery bags in one trip from the car, and instead commissioning my kids, isn't lazy. It's self-aware.

Texting a friend to tell her that today is a rough day isn't whiny. It's healthy and vulnerable.

Fair warning: If you ask for help, people are going to know you need help. They might even know you can't do it all on your own. They might realize you're a normal human and not a superhero. They might think, *Wow, this girl has limits.*

But here's the thing: You *do* need help, you *can't* do it all on your own, you *are* a normal human. You *do* have limits.

And so do I.

During that same season of anxiety, I'd agreed to do a speaking event for Father's Day. As the date came closer, I was too frozen to do anything about it. I'd open my computer to start writing what I wanted to say, and I couldn't think of a single thing. I'd close it quickly and swear to come back to it later. I couldn't even go to Costco to buy chicken without crying. How was I going to stand in front of a group of people and speak?

Every time I thought of contacting the event coordinator and letting them know I couldn't do it, my body would flood with panic, and I'd go into denial. Surely I'd feel better with a little more time. Surely tomorrow I'd open my computer and the words would flow out. But the week kept coming closer and the anxiety just got thicker. Before I knew it, it was just a few days away and I had nothing to say.

We can bullheadedly force ourselves to do more than we're capable of for a long time, but at some point, something's gotta give. A few nights before the event, friends were over for dinner when someone asked how I was feeling about it.

"Um, well," I started, and then the tears began rolling down my face so that I couldn't speak for a while. "I have been so anxious, I have nothing."

She looked up, surprised. I'd given speeches many times before without any issues. My friend put down her fork. "Oh my gosh, I had no idea you were feeling that way. What can we do?"

"Would you guys want to, like, help me?" I asked timidly, more tears falling into my plate of pasta.

"Of course," they said. "Let's make a plan."

Three days later, I got up onstage simply to introduce them, and they stepped in for me, doing the event instead of me. They took turns sharing, telling heartwarming stories about their own dads. They talked about how much they valued the fathers in the room. It ended up being beautiful. I should have asked for help so much sooner, but my friends rescued me despite my stubborn absurdity, and I'll never forget it. The coordinator of the event was surprised, and possibly annoyed, when I told him the change of plans, but afterward he told me how special it ended up being. And to be honest, even if it had turned into a huge train wreck, oh well. I'd still made the right decision. My mental health is more valuable than any one performance.

I'm done pretending.

I can't do it all, guys.

If we don't ask for help, something will snap eventually, whether it's our mental health or our physical health. For me it was both. Before the speech I was supposed to give, there were a hundred things I'd pressed through, a hundred signs I'd ignored, a hundred times I'd told myself "I got this" even though deep down there were warning signs I did not "have this." The CHECK ENGINE light was on and I just kept driving.

When we ask for help, real connection happens. Getting to be there for someone in their time of need builds a special kind of bond that can't come from anything else. I don't know about you, but when I'm vulnerable enough to ask for help (or receive help), it is a direct act of defiance to the story I've told myself that I'm alone. What story do you need to defy today? That you're not worth it? That it's all on you?

Helping and being helped is an essential part of connection. Without it, something will always be missing.

We need one another. Let's stop cheating ourselves out of the privilege it is to need and be needed, to lean on one another and do life truly together.

STEP NINE: Ask for Help When You Need Help

See also: Let people help you when they offer.

Are you the kind of person who is aware of your limits? Or do you go and go until you're on the side of the road wondering why your engine is in flames?

If you're the first, good job. Don't let the pressure from people who don't pace themselves make you feel bad about the way you operate. You're honoring your needs and your limits, and that's healthy. The rest of us need to learn from you, not vice versa.

If you're the latter, I get it. Changing takes practice. Write down a few warning signs you've noticed when you're doing too much or it's time to ask for help, so you can start adjusting earlier and take better care of yourself.

When I'm starting to get out of whack, I start to get critical of other people. I roll my eyes at the annoying man at the grocery store; I grumble to myself about something trivial Graham said or did. This is a sign I'm pushing myself too hard.

I also notice I feel tired when I do things that normally wouldn't make me tired. Hosting is usually really life-giving for me, for example. If people are over and I find myself withdrawing or watching the clock, I know I'm really running on empty and need to recharge.

At that point, I've learned to take a step back and readjust. Is there something I need help with, at home or at work? Am I powering through instead of acknowledging that I'm at the end of my rope?

What about you? Are you carrying too much? Juggling too many balls? Handling too many things on your own?

If the answer is yes, it's time to ask for help.

A LETTER FROM ME

Dear Friend,

No more hiding.

   Figuratively or literally.

   Connection is scary.

   Asking for help is risky.

   But it's worth it.

   You've got this.

               Love,

               Jess

PART THREE

Lies That Keep Us from Dreaming Big and Living a Full Life

(Or, How to Try Things Without Fear of Failure)

LIE #10: I'm a Junior Varsity Adult, and the Best Spot for Me Is Usually the Bench

10/29/2003

Dear Diary,

It is my eighteenth birthday, so I guess I'm an adult now.

I don't feel very adultish.

I guess I'll go pierce my belly button later. Maybe that will help.

Wait, do I have to floss now?

Love,

Jess

've always had this unspoken belief that I'm a junior varsity adult—that I don't have the skills or maturity to make the real team, and it's fine, I'm mostly just here to hang out with my friends anyway. Don't worry, I'll just be over here cheering for everyone else from the sidelines.

I don't know if you've ever watched a high school varsity game after a JV one, but it's kind of like, *Oh, that's how it's supposed to be played.* The varsity adults have careers, they show up at the DMV with all the appropriate forms of ID, and they don't have a mental breakdown trying to understand fourth-grade math. They have different shoes for different activities and probably even remember where they put their keys. If they're a nurse or a police officer, that's an automatic varsity adult badge; don't ask me why. Anyone in a uniform, really. My USPS delivery guy is definitely a varsity adult. Teachers? Automatic varsity. I'm friends with my kid's teacher now, and it's hard for me not to call her Mrs. and feel like I should raise my hand when I talk to her.

Occasionally I meet another junior varsity adult. I recognize them by their dry shampoo and dirty leggings. I'm like, Oh yeah, I see you, we're on the same team for sure. Want to take our kids to McDonald's later? Hopefully we'll get a trophy for participation. We will sit on the bench while the varsity adults do responsible things like head up the PTA and organize bake sales. Someday, if we're lucky, maybe we'll get to join their team. Better yet, maybe they'll look in our direction and give us a pity smile. Together we will be impressed that their hair is done, that they wear grown-up clothes, and that they send out emails to tell us things.

I don't know why I struggle to understand that I'm a complete adult. I'm not lacking, I'm not inferior, I'm not stupid, I'm not an imposter.

The other night, Graham and I went on a date. I was getting ready, trying on jeans and throwing them to the side like they'd personally offended me. I was PMSing and had already apologized for being grumpy not twice, but thrice.

I walked by Graham mumbling to myself.

"Are you sure this is a good night to do this?" he asked.

"Yes, it's great, why?" I said cheerfully.

He raised his eyebrows, and I gave the truthful answer. "Honestly, I just really want those beer queso nachos, and if I don't have them I might cry. Also, once I start eating, I think I'll be fine."

I had a drink and the nachos, and with a mind more at peace,

I started to dissect all the things that were building up in my mind. I told Graham how I'd been struggling with focus. I had a lot of things piling up that I needed to get done, and instead of working on any of it, I'd spent almost five hours researching getaways for no reason at all. "It's just . . . there's so much happening . . ." I said, and that's when I started bawling right there in the restaurant. Which in retrospect is maybe why he asked me if the restaurant was a good idea.

"The kids and school, work, company coming, your birthday, laundry, the kids leaving their socks wedged between the couch cushions . . ." Sometimes a good period cry is where it's at. The feelings are all real; they're just brought to the surface by raging hormones. Sometimes I actually feel sad for boys that they don't have a once-a-month emotional explosion. Not really, but kind of.

The waitress brought us our drinks and cleared the plate of nachos.

"I'm never going to be good at balance, and I really wish I was sometimes." The tears ran down my cheeks. "Everyone is always going to be disappointed in me because this is how I am, and I can keep trying, but I'm never going to be a different person." Suddenly, it felt like every person I'd ever disappointed was sitting right there at the table with us.

"I like who you are," said Graham, leaning back in his chair. I know he does. I like him, too.

The movie *Barbie* has an incredible monologue by America Ferrera that encompasses the impossibility of being a woman. The script, written by Greta Gerwig, begins with this: "It is literally impossible to be a woman. You are so beautiful, and so smart, and it kills me that you don't think you're good enough. Like, we have to always be extraordinary, but somehow we're always doing it wrong."

I feel that, all the way down to my bones, to my soul, to the bottom of my plate of nachos. No matter how we do it, it feels wrong. No matter what our strengths are, we feel like we should have other ones. No matter how much we're slaying in one area, we are acutely aware of our weaknesses.

Ferrera goes on to say a few other things that stand out to me.

"You have to lead, but you can't squash other people's ideas."

"You're supposed to love being a mother, but don't talk about your kids all the damn time."

"You have to be a career woman but also always be looking out for other people."

I don't care who you are. I don't care if you're a teacher, a stay-at-home mom, an actress, or Taylor Swift, I can guarantee you've felt the pressure because it's universal.

A couple of years ago, I got diagnosed with ADHD, and a lot of things that I never really understood about myself started to make sense. Knowing a little bit more about how my brain worked gave me so much more understanding about things that always seemed like weird quirks: my forgetfulness, my lack of attention to detail, and my seeming inability to be balanced.

I do this thing with hyperfocus. Whatever my attention is on at a given time completely captivates me. I forget everything else. If it's work, I can get a ton of stuff done at once. If it's a person, that person will feel like the queen or king of the universe because I won't just be a good friend, I'll be the greatest most incredible friend that has ever existed. If it's anxiety, everything is very bad and there is nothing else. I usually can bring about three things into my focus at a time, and I've learned to implement rituals to fill in the gaps. For example, I set a twenty-minute timer reminding me to clean the kitchen each morning. That way, I don't have to use any of my brain power, I just do it. I always put my keys in the same drawer because my brain doesn't remember boring things like where I set them.

I once heard someone explain that operating outside your natural strengths is like putting a rubber band on your thumb and pointer finger and then holding them apart. You can do it, you're capable, but over time it'll cause tension because it's a literal stretch for you.

I'm acutely aware of the things I need to work on, and I do, but I'm never going to be a different human entirely, and I don't want to be.

I saw a viral post recently that caught my attention. Someone posted, "Hey kids who got 'talks too much' on their report cards in elementary school, what are you doing now?" Most of the responses were things like keynote speaker, lawyer, counselor, radio personality, or sales. Things that absolutely made sense. Sometimes we're too much in the classroom, because we're meant to be somewhere else.

Another person asked the question, "Everyone that had 'too quiet' on your report cards as a kid. What are you doing for a job now?" Among the nearly seven thousand responses were jobs like teacher, social worker, therapist, and nurse. The creator of the post noted that over 50 percent of the responders were in some kind of caregiving career, and someone else pointed out that many of them became the people they needed when they were little.

Someone else posted on Reddit, "People who shoved their school papers in their backpack with no binder/folder etc., where are you now?" The post had over twenty-one thousand responses. My favorite part is that after listing their occupation, almost everyone added that their organizational style hadn't changed. They said things like:

> "I'm an engineer. My desk is cluttered with loose papers and pens."
> "Just started my PhD program, currently shoving papers in my backpack."

"I'm a nurse, now I shove my papers in drawers."

"Manage a hedge fund with my desk covered in paper."

The truth is, we all have shortcomings and weaknesses, especially if we're looking for them, but we also have superpowers.

I talked to a woman once who'd worked alongside one of the most influential people in the world—someone who created organizations that changed millions of lives, a person who inspired greatness from the largest stages. This woman's boss was a "real" adult, if we believed in that (we don't, remember). I asked her what it was like, and she said, "Oh they're a wonderful person, very inspiring, but I definitely would never want to be married to them."

I laughed, surprised. "Why not?"

"They're very intense all the time. They're never not 'on,' ya know? They're just go-go-go all the time."

I think she made an interesting point. Sometimes we look at people who are confidently operating in their strengths, who clearly are doing the thing they were born to do, and we assume they don't have weaknesses. That's not true. Turns out (according to my friend) they're not all that much fun. But also, so what? They're them. They're leaning hard into how they were wired, and they're not asking permission to be themselves; that's inspiring. We can do the exact same thing, but in our own unique set of strengths.

No one is doing it all. Read that again. No one is doing it all because "it all" is impossible, absolutely positively impossible. You're not on the junior varsity team, and you're not the only one on the varsity team who's pretending. The standards are a joke. We don't feel like grown-ups, we don't feel like "real" adult women, because there aren't any.

I'm bad at a lot of things. (We talked about that in chapter 1.)

This morning it took me thirty minutes to find socks that match. I worry about real things and highly unlikely things with the same amount of passion. I'm just over here stressing about getting ready for a trip we have coming up, and also what if when we go through airport security I accidentally bring a large knife? Like I'm making dinner and I get confused and toss the bread knife in my carry-on instead of the kitchen cupboard?

I'm also good at a lot. And so are you.

Your list of things you're bad at and good at might be similar to what I shared, or we might be polar opposites. Maybe you're amazing at being organized and balance is something you excel at, but you have that other list, too—the one saying that showing affection is hard for you, and when someone you love is going through a crisis you feel lost on how to be there for them. You gave them a hug, but you're pretty sure you pulled away too fast and crap, you made it weird. Or maybe it says that creativity is a stretch, and drawing stick figures is going to be about as good as it gets for you.

It really doesn't matter what's on your lists. What I'm telling you is that you're enough. That the world needs you at the plate doing your thing, whatever that thing may be, because there's no other you.

I have a son who absolutely doesn't bring his shoes anywhere we go. I remember driving to the grocery store with all the kids when he was about eight years old. It was snowing outside as I pulled the youngest out of her car seat and buckled her into the shopping cart. "Okay, let's go, guys!" I said, grabbing my purse.

"Um, Mom, do I need shoes?" He peered at me from the back seat.

"Yessss," I said, hoping this did not mean what I thought it meant. "Did you bring your shoes?"

"I didn't know I needed shoes."

I pictured him walking barefoot to the car in the snow before we left. "For the record, anytime we go to the store, you should bring your shoes."

He grinned sheepishly. "No one told me."

"Okay, I'm telling you now, and this will cover the rest of all eternity: Bring your shoes to the grocery store, 'kay? Also, when you walk from the house to the car in the snow, shoes are a yes."

A few days ago I asked if both of my boys wanted to go get lunch with me at one of our favorite restaurants. They would literally eat a vat of pasta and a side of beef at any given time day or night, so the answer was, of course, yes.

When we got there, I started to open the car door when I heard his now much deeper voice from the back seat: "Was I supposed to bring shoes?"

He is fifteen years old. My other son and I teased him incessantly (because at this point it's become a theme), and we sat outside to eat because at least it wasn't snowing.

This kid is constantly surprised. Surprised by getting up in the morning. Surprised by school. Surprised about brushing his hair.

He is a free spirit, an old soul, and a gift of comedic relief. He is incredibly witty, creative, and gifted at thinking outside of the box. He is kindhearted and thoughtful. He doesn't give a crap about wearing colors that match, but I'm 100 percent positive this kid is going places. He is a gift to the world, a gift to me, and a gift to everyone who knows him, exactly how he is.

I can't wait to see what he does.

Each and every one of us has a different set of strengths and weaknesses, and every single one of us is just as qualified as the others. I think the trick is to be delighted. To be delighted by one another and all the ways we are unique, and delighted by ourselves, too.

Listen, you are the star hitter of your life and your story, and

I'm the star hitter of mine. You're bad at hitting home runs? No problem; this game is won by ground balls and stealing bases. Whatever it is you *are* good at is exactly what is needed for your life. You are the varsity, CEO, captain, chief, queen, and president.

**STEP TEN: Believe That You Are Qualified
Just as You Are**

Is there an area in your life where you feel like you're on the junior varsity team?

Speak this over yourself and let it seep into your core:

I am qualified to:

_____

(for example, be an adult, parent my kids, lead this team, do this job).

I will never be able to do it all, but I'm pretty dang awesome just as I am.

My strengths and my weaknesses do not make me better or worse than anyone else.

I struggle with:

_____

_____

_____

And that's okay. I can learn and I can grow, but I will also accept myself as I am.

I am awesome at:

_____

_____

_____

Read through the next sentences. If one or two resonate, make it your mantra in the coming weeks.

I am qualified.

My voice matters.

I'm not an imposter.

My opinion is important.

I have the power to change things in my life that I want to change.

I will work on being the best version of *me*, not on being perfect.

LIE #11: It's Better Not to Try Than to Mess Up in Front of Everyone

- - - - - - - - - -

Dear God,

I have a piano recital tonight, and I'm going to need your holy angels to come keep me from hitting that note with my rogue pinkie.

This is basically the pinnacle of my life, and if I embarrass myself I am going to move to a new town.

I will also need God's holy angels to make sure I don't forget to wear pants at my recital.

Amen.

Love,

Jess

I n my late twenties, I got asked to speak at my little community church in Montana. I was honored to be asked, and I had zero worries until it came to the morning of, wherein I turned into a basket case who'd never wanted to do this in the first place and why did I even say yes and this was the worst idea I've ever had in my entire adult life. Graham made eggs and nodded while I verbally vomited the breakdown that was happening in my head. I was just wondering *why* he'd let me say yes to this and did he think that maybe I was getting sick because I didn't feel good and I absolutely, beyond a shadow of a doubt, *could not do this.* He slid a coffee across the table and told me I could, and also he was going to go put pants on now.

By the time we got to church I was feeling better. I'd dealt with my anxiety by adding caffeine to it, and now I was jittery enough to mistake fear for excitement. All through the music and announcements, I felt like a competitive sprinter waiting for the sound of the starting gun. *Just let me go, just let me up there, let's get this over with.* The pastor took the mic and, to be honest with you, I'm not really sure it was time, but my legs started taking me there anyway. I ran/jogged up to meet him, but as I jumped up on the platform, my foot caught something and instead of making the graceful entrance I'd planned, I launched over the stage like Eddie the Eagle. I caught a significant amount of air before crashing on all fours, surrounded by cords and speakers.

The room went dead quiet. It was then that my husband realized he should have taken my rant more seriously and let me stay in bed. I picked myself up, took the mic, and looked out upon the stunned crowd of about 150 people, most of them family and friends. They frantically avoided eye contact with me as they picked fuzz off their sweaters and dug in their purses for imaginary pens.

I took a deep breath, noting that my knees were definitely bruised, and then I burst out laughing. "Can we just take a moment," I wheezed, "to laugh at that?"

Like a balloon that finally popped, the room erupted into hysteria. We tried to pull ourselves together, but it was almost impossible, and now we were basically bonded for life.

I've spoken quite a few times since then, but you want to know something? That first time was one of my favorites. One, because it taught me to relax, and taught me that even if I embarrass myself, it's going to be okay. Two, because it showed me that I'd much rather make people laugh than impress them. I'm like Buddy the elf, except instead of smiling it's laughing. I would have tripped over the stage on purpose if I knew it was going to be such a crowd pleaser. (Kidding. Kind of . . .)

I don't know about you, but it's not just stages I'm scared of messing up on. I'm scared of taking new risks in my career. I'm scared of messing up in my marriage and as a mother. I'm scared of pursuing that new friendship with the girl who seems way too cool for me. I'm scared of taking that class at the gym because what if I look like a red, sweaty mess and can't keep up? (Okay, that one happened.) I'm scared of letting myself set big goals, because what if I don't reach them?

It can be absolutely paralyzing. One of my friends was so scared of becoming a mother (and failing her kids) that she put it off and put it off, even though she wanted it deeply. Another friend avoided all long-term relationships because she didn't believe she was capable of healthy commitment, even though that was all her heart desired. One more is the most talented person I know, but for a long time she sabotaged every opportunity to advance her career because it was so scary to risk the disappointment of reality when she could stay safe in the dream of possibility. That crap is real. It's very, very real.

The truth is, we may fall on our face. We may launch over that stage like an Olympic ski jumper (you probably won't, but let me imagine this is an "us" problem, 'kay?). We may fail. We will definitely make mistakes. We will face disappointments.

What if we started doing a better job at honoring our own bravery for facing our fears and stepping into the realm of I-might-bomb-but-I'm-going-to-try-it-anyway? What if we started treating life more like a karaoke bar and less like an audition for *The Voice*?

I'm a people person. I like pretty much everyone except a few contestants on *Survivor* who shall remain nameless. If you are one of those naturally poised and together people, I have nothing but admiration, but there is a special place in my heart for the ones who roll into the school drop-off wearing a big hoodie because a bra just wasn't happening that morning, looking like they're currently contestants on *Survivor* living off rainwater and adrenaline. I see you and I love you, because I am you.

I'm tired of the idea that we should tiptoe into our life and hope we don't mess it up. It's *our* life. We should walk into it confidently.

I will never forget holding my firstborn son in my arms in a sterile hospital room on a Sunday night. I'd packed my hospital bag fifteen times in the month before his due date, but every time I loaded up my underwear, my toothbrush, and my favorite sweats, I remembered I needed to use them again. (I've never been quite sure how the go-bag is supposed to work. Do y'all buy more underwear than you need? Have a second pair of favorite sweats on hand? Splurge on multiple toothbrushes? Please explain.)

I sat there in the dark while my husband snored softly on a vinyl teal couch across the room. I held our newborn at my chest, trying to remember the way the nurse told me to get him to latch, biting my bottom lip to fight the pain. Finally he was nursing. I stared at his soft skin, his small features, his wispy hair. I tried to decide if his nose was from my side or Graham's side, and if it was too big for his face. He was cradled there in my arms like an open invitation. An invitation to do the most high-stakes thing I'd ever done. An invitation to love someone more than I loved myself. An invitation to do life scared. An invitation to be more than I thought I could be. Motherhood is crazy like that.

I soaked up those days in the hospital like they were a short vacation—if vacations involved a throbbing nether region, newborn pamper ice packs (for me), and finally learning the use of witch hazel. On day three, it was time to go home, and Graham went to get the car seat still covered in tags. I brushed my hair and got dressed, and the nurse came in to check that we'd buckled in our newborn correctly. "All right," she said. "You're good to go!"

"Great!" I said, but on the inside I could feel panic welling up. There was no way we were ready for this. There was no way we were qualified to walk out of this hospital with a human child. Did they know that I was always losing my debit card? Did they know that I sometimes forgot to brush my teeth? Did they know that I wasn't an actual qualified medical professional?

"Bye!" she said cheerfully. "Congratulations!"

Graham grabbed the car seat and I thought, *Is he insane? Surely he knows this is a terrible idea.*

But we left.

The next day I was sitting on my mother-in-law's couch in a fog when she handed me back the baby and asked, "Has your milk come in yet?"

"Come again?" I said. Milk "come in"? What the heck did that mean? If I didn't have milk, why the heck was this kid spending so much time terrorizing my nipples?

"Your milk, did it come in?"

"What does that mean?"

"Well, first you have colostrum, and then after a few days the milk comes in."

"Colo-huh? Well, I guess I don't know."

"You'll know," she said.

That night I knew. My milk came in, all right. It came in like a wrecking ball. To this day my boob skin is marked by the memories of the night they graduated from a B to a triple FFF. Those suckers were the size of my head, and unfortunately for my husband, I became a sex icon at the precise time when I never wanted to be touched ever again. I didn't know what to do with them, and neither did my baby, because there was no "hamburgering" those tatas; they were made of solid steel. Both the baby and I just looked at them and cried. Well, I cried, and the baby screamed. Apparently he didn't enjoy the fire hose of milk that had now replaced "colostrum."

I stood in front of the mirror staring at myself, weeping because they were so impressive, but also so painful. I handed Graham the baby and called the maternity ward to explain that they'd let me go too early. Through my sobs I told the nurse on the phone about my giant boob problem. "It's okay, honey," she said, perfectly sweet and calm. "Are you bringing baby to breast or breast to baby?" and just like that, she solved all my problems. Miracle worker, I tell you.

My oldest is in high school now, and he has three younger siblings following close behind. Some things got easier with each baby, some got harder, and it turns out I hardly ever know what I'm doing. Those nurses forgot to tell me that every year would bring new stages, and each and every kid would be completely different from the others. They didn't give me a road map because there isn't one.

My kids see me at my best and they see me at my worst. I snuggle them, I hug them, I whisper "I love you." (Sometimes I obnoxiously shout "*I love you and I think you're amazing!*" until they laugh and roll their eyes and tell me to stop.) I stare at them when I think they're not looking and am in awe of who they are—until they catch me and say, "Mom, you're looking at me like that again." I pick up one million socks per day and tell myself they're worth it. I walk into their rooms at night and I pray over them that God will protect their precious hearts and empower them toward their dreams. I also lecture too much and I'm grumpy in the mornings. I get impatient, and sometimes I snap when I should be sensitive. Sometimes I dole out chores when what they need is a hug. I tell them to stop arguing when I really should have taken a moment to listen. When I've picked up one sock too many, I lose my ever-loving mind over a smelly Hanes crew stuck between the cushions of the couch. I can't tell you how many times I've sat beside them and said, "Hey, I'm sorry. I had a bad attitude today and I got it wrong. I'm sorry for being a jerk."

The truth is, I'm just one mess of a mama who apologizes often and loves my kids with every fiber of my being. I don't really know what I'm doing any more than I did when the nurse stuck two fingers under the belt of our brand-new infant car seat to check if it was tight enough. Every single stage brings me into the new and unknown. Right now, my kids are stinky and hormonal, and I can't say that's easier than cracked nipples and sleepless nights. All I can do is trust my gut and keep telling them to put on deodorant. All I can do is show up in the arena with an open heart and an open mind and leave absolutely everything I have on the dirt floor that is motherhood. All I can do is apologize when I get it wrong. Sometimes I might fall on my face, but I'll never regret giving it my all.

There is a woman named Tenzin Kiyosaki who has been a hospice chaplain in Los Angeles for over a decade, caring for people who have less than six months to live and listening to their concerns. She wrote a book about her experiences, and in an interview with the *Today* show, she said that the number one regret her patients share with her is, *I did not live the life of my dreams.* One woman always wanted to travel and didn't. Others said they wished they applied for their dream job or moved to a new city.

I want to be clear, though: Showing up in your own life doesn't always mean doing the things that look "impressive" or "fancy." Sure, maybe I'm talking about speaking at that thing, writing that book, going for that promotion, running for office, or going back to school for that degree, but I'm also talking about showing up in motherhood, fully aware that we're going to make billions of mistakes. I'm talking about standing at the altar knowing that there is never a guarantee that the person we've given our heart to won't also break it, or that we won't break theirs. I'm talking about walking in the door of counseling scared half to death of the feelings we don't feel prepared to feel. I'm talking about risking friendship when we've been hurt and betrayed. I'm talking about having a hard conversation with someone we love deeply, even though they might be hurt or angry.

Not everyone wants to speak on a stage or become a mom, but we all have things that scare us, and those things are gatekeeping parts of our heart that matter. Let's not regret the things we didn't try.

STEP ELEVEN: Failure Shmailure

What do you want to try, but you're scared you'll fail at it?

Make a list of two or three things. Is it travel? Starting a business? Committing in a relationship?

What is something you can do that will be a step toward trying?

You are never going to be perfect. You're not. But you're always going to be the perfect person to live your life, fully, wholeheartedly, messily, brokenly. I for one am going to celebrate you every single time you enter the arena. Win, lose, doesn't matter. Look how freaking brave you are.

LIE #12: I Can't Do That Because No One Does That

9/10/1996

Dear Diary,

I have to wear a dress to church today because my mom says it's nice to wear dresses to church. Plus my aunt bought it, and we don't want it to go to waste.

I would rather walk across hot coals than wear this thing because it makes my armpits itchy and tree climbing impossible. Also there's no dumber thing I could possibly have on, unless I enjoyed losing at tag and worrying about showing my underwear.

Love,

Jess

O ne time I shaved my head.

I'll back up . . .

There was a doll in the 1980s called the Dolly Surprise. When you raised her right arm, her hair would grow instantaneously. I never owned that doll, but I was highly invested in her commercials that came on while I was watching Saturday-morning cartoons.

My hair grows just like Dolly Surprise: fast and thick in what seems like days. When I was a kid, it hung down to my hips, brown and silky with natural blond highlights from the sun. It was the thing people always noticed first about me. "Wow, your hair is so long!" "Wow, your hair is so thick and beautiful!" Strangers would come up to me in the grocery store and tell me, "Don't ever cut your hair."

I guess I've never liked being told what to do. As soon as I was old enough, I started cutting my hair. I dyed it often. I kept up the habit all through high school and early adulthood, but when I was twenty-six and had just had Scout, my second baby, my Dolly Surprise hair had come in thick and long again. Once again, it became the thing people noticed first. "Wow, your hair!" If I said something about cutting it, their response was always, "Oh no, don't ever cut it!"

So yeah, I decided I wanted to shave it.

I had this really cool hairstylist who had shaved her head twice, and, I don't know, it just seemed like a good time. I had a two-year-old and a three-month-old, and I was severely lacking in good times. I needed a little wild in my life, and there was zero cost for buzzing my head.

Everyone knows you've got to take the big risks before you talk yourself out of them and before your mom hears what you're thinking, so one night I commissioned Graham to shave it. (He had visions of G.I. Jane and was like, "Yeah, cool, let's do it.") There we were, in the bathroom after the kids had gone to bed, giggling as we watched my long hair fall to the ground. You don't really know if you have a good head or a bad head until after your hair is gone, but lucky for me, I have a good one, I guess. I'm not sure what my backup plan was. Probably gluing my hair back on like I used to try with my Barbies.

I think I wanted to do it so badly because I knew that I fell into a certain box: stereotypical mom who loves shopping at Target and watching reality TV. No one told me, *You're not allowed to shave your head,* but I felt it. Moms do not go around buzzing their heads, and that's exactly why I wanted to do it. That night I couldn't stop staring in the mirror. I kept feeling my stubbly head. Did I like it? Graham and I laughed nervously together, like what on earth had we just done? Suddenly I became acutely aware of how long it would be before I had long hair again. I felt naked and vulnerable without it. Neither of us regretted it, but we did both secretly cry ourselves to sleep.

Sometimes it feels like there's this giant book of rules we're supposed to follow. I picture it heavy and covered in dust, maybe sitting in a hidden temple like the one from *Indiana Jones.* It's been there for ages, and we don't usually ask questions; we just try to live by this code. We say that we love ourselves, that we want to be free and healthy, but there's this standard lingering in the backs of our minds that causes us to question our own thoughts and ideas.

The next morning we were going to church, and I asked Graham if I should wear a hat, rubbing my head nervously. "No, you should rock it and rock it proudly, it looks awesome." So I put on earrings and heels, and we set off. The shock factor was everything I'd hoped for. Friends gasped. My mother-in-law exclaimed and told me she loved it. Little kids stared at me with their mouths hanging open. It felt like an act of defiance to the rule book.

Would I do it again? No. The mullet stage is rough unless you're a mullet type of person. But it empowered me in just the way I needed back then, and it was an adventure when other adventures were limited.

What I am saying is that sometimes we've got to listen to the sound of our own hearts above any other noise. Sometimes when we feel trapped inside an invisible fence, we've got to just bulldoze it a little to remind ourselves who's boss. Just because people *don't* doesn't mean you *can't*. Just because there are lines to color inside, it doesn't mean you can't go wild with the crayon.

I'm just guessing, but I think it's a natural human thing to want to put people in boxes so we can understand them. We do it in our families and we do it to our friends, expecting them to stay who we've always known them to be. Graham is one of six kids, for example. They're all over thirty-seven and yet they'll always be known to one another as things like "the one who is always brushing her teeth," "the one who always says the hike is shorter than it is," and "the one who cries when weeding." His sister is a grown adult. I'm pretty sure she no longer cries when weeding.

Outside of our families, we have group parameters. These are expectations for what group members do. The consequences for stepping out of line are made clear by the flood of whispers and headshaking when someone dares question the narrative. Maybe it's a family, maybe it's a church, maybe it's a whole community. These are things like:

No one moves out of our hometown.
Everyone goes to this church.
We all vote _____.
We all believe _____ on this certain issue.

Best-case scenario, we're surprised when someone does things differently. Worst case, we reject them for being "other."

The thing is, we weren't meant to grow in small pots forever. We were meant to be planted in the ground, where our roots have room to spread out and we can get as big and tall as we're able. We were never meant to stop evolving and changing. We were never meant to follow all the rules.

My mom was a true cowgirl when she met my dad. She barrel

raced, led trail rides, and trained horses. She got along better with the surly old cowboys that she worked with in the stables than she ever did with the girls at her high school. She was wildly independent and felt happiest when she was in the mountains with her horse. She and my dad were only fifteen when they met. They planned to be ranch hands until they could afford their own ranch someday.

Plans changed, as they often do, and at twenty-seven she was a pastor's wife instead, raising two kids. She soon discovered that there were a lot of expectations that came with the role: things like hosting ladies' luncheons and playing the piano at church. People were disappointed when she didn't start a women's ministry or take them out to coffee to discuss their marriages. But that's just not who she was.

All my life, people have been telling me my mom is so sweet, and she is, but here's the thing you need to know about Susan: She's also feisty as heck, and no one is going to tell Susan what to do. She won't be rude about it. She will make cookies or bake a cake to bring on Sunday, and she'll hang out with your kids and read them stories or teach them a craft in Sunday school. But she's not going to play the piano or host any luncheons, and if you put her on a committee she will say, "Thanks for thinking of me," and get right back off that committee. I love that about my mom. She's beautiful, gracious, and kind, and she's also wild and untamed.

Let's be like Susan.

You're the only one who knows how to be authentically you. You're the only one who can push against the boundaries and say nope. You're the only one who can tap into that little girl inside who, once upon a time, planted her toddler feet solidly in that olive-green shag carpet, placed her hands on her hips, and said "*No*" when she was told to brush her teeth. There was a time to listen to the adults in our lives, but guess what, you're an adult now, too (the varsity kind, remember?), and you get a say. You get the main say, actually.

Here are a few rules I've personally decided to break:

Any rules about what you're allowed to wear at a "certain age." There was an article published years back listing a bunch of clothes you should no longer wear if you're above thirty. I immediately set off to buy scrunchies, graphic tees, and sparkly pants (all apparently off-limits). See also articles that instruct what you "cannot wear if you have curves," or what you "cannot wear if you don't have curves." Ex-squeeze me, magazine writers: I will wear what I please. Opinions unwelcome.

Cooking on medium and low. This is some BS cookbooks try to boss me around with, and I want it to be known that I will be cooking on high because ain't nobody got time for that. (Yes, I know most people have time for that. I am who I am.) See also: things that are not dishwasher-safe or have to be dry-cleaned. I have enough drama in my life. My food, clothes, and dishes do not get to be drama queens.

Buying gifts for (or apologizing in general to) people on airplanes for the torture of having to exist in the same space as my children. Lord have mercy. I get that it can be obnoxious, but this is public transportation. Children are a normal part of society, and you're actually not entitled to an adult-only flight unless you pay for it. So put on your noise-canceling headphones and enjoy your life. I will do my best to comfort them and keep them from crying, I will apologize profusely if they kick your seat, and I will do my best not to inconvenience you in any way. But also, I bought six tickets to your one, sorry not sorry.

Then there are the "rules" that make my skin crawl:

When a strange man in a bar told me I should "smile more," because I didn't accept his advances.
When I'm told that my work is inside the home.
When I'm told that's not "ladylike."
When someone says women shouldn't be in charge. Gross.
When a stranger on the internet told me I can't be a Christian because I swear.
When someone chooses to use their public platform to condemn a person's lifestyle and the people who affirm them.

Excuse me while I get theological here, but there are 194 scriptures about loving people. There are more than 2,000 scriptures on poverty and justice. There are 365 scriptures about not being afraid. I believe you might be lopsided.

Look, I'm not suggesting we go entirely feral and start showing up to work without pants (unless you work from home, because that would be awesome). There are laws for a reason, and there are rules that make sense. But some rules feel like putting on an underwire bra—even if you can put up with it, you can't wait to take that thing off at the end of the day.

If you find yourself operating within parameters you don't feel are entirely right for you, if you find yourself holding back to make other people more comfortable, if your inner voice is questioning why, it's time to trust your gut and have a rule shakedown. Are you okay with being passed over for a promotion even though you're more than qualified? Are you okay with the way that pastor talks about women? Are you okay with the division of household chores in your home? Are you okay with the way the people around you talk about racism?

I'm convinced that every single one of us is meant to outgrow the dirt we were originally planted in, no matter how good and wonderful that space is. So let yourself grow, let yourself be. Remind yourself who is the boss of you.

As women, we're already walking a path that was laid by other women who refused to obey the rules; women who said, "Nope, I don't think men will be making all the decisions actually, women are going to vote and we're going to change the world." What if they all chose to exist within normal and safe? What if they never challenged the way things were always done?

It's about you and it's about me, but it's also much bigger than us. It's about breaking the rules for our daughters and our sons. It's about breaking the rules for the women who don't have the strength or ability to do it themselves. It's about living freely.

It's not about doing something crazy. It's about making sure you're doing the right thing for you—especially if that happens to fall outside the lines that most people color inside. Be like Susan. Don't get on any committees you don't feel like being on. Don't play the dang piano if you don't wanna. Don't break your own spirit. You weren't meant to be tame, you were meant to be you.

STEP TWELVE: Break the Box and Let Yourself Be You

What boxes might you be inside?

Where do they come from? Do they come from family, friends, society, or church?

What feels right and good, and what feels ill fitting and burdensome?

Sometimes we're so used to living within certain parameters, it's hard to even see them there. It might take a bit of digging and soul-searching. It might take some questioning of why you do the things you've always done. But you, my friend, are valuable, and your thoughts, your needs, your ideas are valuable. It's okay if you're outgrowing the ground you were planted in.

Seven years ago, we started to feel an itch to move. We loved our hometown; we loved the people in it. We loved our families and we loved our routines, but something about it wasn't fitting anymore, and there was a deep restlessness we couldn't shake. To be honest, there was grief in it, too. I wanted the things that had always fit to still fit, but there was also a deeper sense of adventure and excitement about what was to come. We knew something needed to change, and as we talked, the thing we landed on was this:

"We don't know exactly where we're going, but we know we can't stay here."

When you think of outgrowing your current surroundings, what comes to mind?

For us, it was an actual physical move that transplanted us to a new state and a community that would challenge us by stretching us outside of all that was familiar and forcing us to grow new roots. It might not be a physical move for you, but the idea stands. Ask yourself if the space you're in currently feels comfortable, or if there is something in it that feels restrictive. It could be a belief system, it could be unspoken family rules, it could be your own insecurity keeping you small. It's okay to start with this:

"I don't know exactly where I'm going, but I know I cannot stay here."

LIE #13: If I Can't Go Big, I Should Just Go Home

<hr/>

12/10/2018

Dear Diary,

When the world is hard and sad and scary, I want to act. I want to change it. I want to do something with my life that matters for more than just myself. I think about all the things I could do . . . and then sometimes I get so overwhelmed and tired, I watch Netflix.

Like, I want to change the world, and I want my life to matter, but I also want to sit here and eat cheese. Does that make sense?

Love,

Jess

Years ago, I had gotten a moment to myself to run to Target on my own. My kids were still little, and I usually had a cart full of small children. Someone was always begging for something: candy, a toy, a colorful box of tampons that they spotted, a trinket from the dollar aisle. My youngest, who is full of fire (and will likely be the first woman president, so watch out), would go full level-ten tantrum, screaming, thrashing, clawing nearly every time we went.

I loved Target so much, my naïve little heart would expect

a different result every time. It never was. I perfected the mother-versus-toddler walk of shame and grew very gifted at the under-the-arm hold, the bear hold, and the one-hand-keeping-her-in-the-cart-seat-while-racing-for-the-Target-exit hold. On a good day, my other three kids would follow dutifully behind me, but on most days one or three of them would be crying about something else. Every single time I felt like bawling. I was so embarrassed, so overwhelmed, and mostly I felt incredibly, acutely alone.

Today was different. On this day, all on my own, breathing in the sweet Target air, I felt like I might have entered heaven on earth. I held a steaming cup of Starbucks in my hand. I lingered in the clothing aisle and reveled at the thought, *I can try stuff on if I want.* (If you've ever sweated your way through a breastfeeding and swimsuit-trying-on session, you know.) I smelled the candles. I perused the home goods and lusted after new throw pillows. There was a hop in my step as I glided toward the checkout, feeling like I'd just had a day at the spa.

Then I noticed the woman standing in line ahead of me. Her four children were having a group meltdown. One wanted to be held, one was sobbing over a candy bar, and one had collapsed to the ground in front of the cart. The mother was frantically digging through her wallet trying to get out her card when I saw that she had a brand-new infant in her arms, wailing.

The empathy I felt in that moment cannot possibly be measured. I longed to jump in, but I didn't even know how. I was a stranger who looked childless at the moment. I tried to think of what I'd want to hear. I smiled reassuringly at her, hoping that she knew that I wasn't judging her or questioning her, but I was with her in solidarity with every ounce of my mama heart. She smiled grimly at me. The college-aged cashier continued to ask her clueless questions. "Would you like to sign up for rewards?"

Does it look like this woman wants rewards? I thought. *Unless you want to reward her with childcare and a margarita, stand down.*

Suddenly she turned to me desperately, her arms full of wailing infant. My looks of solidarity must have translated, because she held the baby out. "I'm sorry, can you hold her for me?"

"Oh my gosh, yes." I dropped my keys and coffee into the cart and took that baby like she was the most precious treasure on earth. I hummed and rocked her, I gave her a paci as Mama knelt to talk to her other kids then finished paying for her stuff. I honestly can't tell you the healing that happened to me in that moment—being able to show up for this mom, being invited to help. All the loneliness I'd ever felt as the mom with four crying kids bubbled to the surface in that moment. I could suddenly see myself with a bird's-eye view. I wasn't alone, not really. I had never been alone.

As the order finished, she turned to me and said, "Thank you." I handed her that baby and we locked eyes for a moment before she walked out of the store. I never saw her again.

There are things we do in life that don't feel very important or significant. At that point in life, I was mostly a stay-at-home mom, picking up coffee shop jobs on the side but usually just trying to get on top of an endless list of to-dos. Things like: make my house not look like a frat house, go grocery shopping, make a dent in the laundry, et cetera.

Every ten minutes there'd be an interruption. They needed a snack, they couldn't find their favorite stuffy, one of them took the other one's blanket, the littlest one's diaper smelled horrific, someone dropped my phone in the toilet. On the productive days, though, it didn't matter what was thrown at me, I stayed the course. The kitchen was my domain, the living room was my realm, and things were about to get whipped into shape. I was sweating, I was exhausted, but dang it, this house was about to be beautiful. Finally I would finish, everything would be in its place, and I'd proudly survey my accomplishment. Sweet success. Who was I? Joanna stinking Gaines? My house looked amazing.

And then, right on cue, and completely predictably, someone would spill something, and that's when all hell would break loose. The youngest would wander out from her nap sobbing, God knows why. I'd realize it was time to make dinner, the boys would sneak up behind me emptying their buckets of Legos on the ground, and Oaklee would walk out of her room with her colored markers and papers, shedding glitter as she bounced. By the time Graham walked in the door, it looked as if I'd just decided that if you can't beat them, join them, and thrown the rest of their toys and granola bar wrappers around the living room.

I'd tell him defeatedly, "It looked amazing in here a few minutes ago." It's not that he was judging me; it was that I was longing to be seen. Longing for someone, anyone, to witness my work. At the end of the day, there was not one single thing I had done that remained "did," and gosh, I felt inconsequential.

Social media brings the whole world into our homes, showing us the highlight reels of everyone else's life. It makes big careers seem normal, celebrity lifestyles seem attainable, and, if we're not careful, it can make every single thing we do seem small and unimportant.

What I've learned, though, and believe with all my heart is that there isn't greater importance in speaking on stages, influencing thousands on Instagram, or kicking butt in a high-profile career. It seems like it, but there really isn't. Sometimes the most thankless jobs are the most meaningful—maybe not in the work, but in the why. My husband has owned a service and cleaning company for years. He has scrubbed windows when it was so cold he had to put antifreeze in the water to keep it from glassing over. He's scrubbed toilets, mopped floors, and performed jobs that are too gross to mention. He doesn't love it. Every single thing he does gets undone again. He doesn't come home glowing about the privilege of squeegeeing someone's ridiculously high French-pane windows or getting attacked by bees on someone's cedar shake roof. But he does it for us. He does it for his family, and you can't tell me for one second that he has less purpose than someone who commutes to a high-profile job in a suit. Likewise, you can't tell me that someone who goes to a desk job with a sense of purpose is less important than a celebrity on TV. It's the thankless things we do for the sake of people we love that really, really matter.

In the last few years, things have changed, and I've had the special privilege of some career wins. When my first book hit the bestseller list, it was amazing. When my co-author Amy and I got invited on *Good Morning America,* it was surreal. My work is no longer invisible to the wider world—but there is nothing about it that matters more than waking up in the middle of the night with my nine-year-old who has had a bad dream, or smoothing the hair back from sweaty foreheads when my kids have the flu. There is nothing less significant or important about my husband's faithfulness and determination, building his company by his own sweat. Someday when I look back on my life, I have a feeling those career moments will make me smile: *What an adventure!* But it will be the other stuff that deeply matters to my heart.

I never want to lose sight of that.

I never want to be a person who thinks that public wins are more important than cooking dinner for my family or taking my friend out for her birthday.

If you are stuck feeling like the things you do are unimportant, narrow your focus. Stop looking through the lens of every-thing and look up close. Who are you loving? Who are you doing it all for? Maybe it's the grandma you visit on the weekends, maybe it's a sister you called on Thursday, or maybe it's your kids and spouse. Maybe it's just simply that you're doing the thing in front of you right now, and even though you don't know exactly where it's leading, there is honor in that.

There is no small, there is no unimportant. There are just people doing their best.

I always used to think that living a meaningful life was about the big stuff. Join the Peace Corps. Found an orphanage. Become Mother Teresa. All those things are amazing, but maybe ill fitting, particularly when I'm raising my own "small football team" (as I was told by one Italian man). I've started focusing on the small moments that pull us out of our own narratives and into someone else's. A man on his way to work stopping to have a conversation with a homeless man and listening to his life story. Buying the food for the person behind you in line. A soccer team turning up for the birthday of a boy with special needs because no one else came. Strangers stopping to help someone push their broken-down car out of the intersection.

We get trapped saying things like, "I just wish I was wealthy so I could help people"; "I just wish I had a bigger house so I could invite them to stay until they get on their feet"; "I just wish I had the time to help." The truth is, you do. Every single little bit changes the world. Thinking about what we can't give keeps us from noticing what we can.

You know what's something that affects your community quickly and effectively? Something that gives you an opportunity to bless someone who isn't normally a part of your circle? Tipping well. It's a simple opportunity to be generous to an actual human being. I have worked in coffee shops and restaurants, and I have seen my co-workers wipe away tears after a single extravagant tip. You can't change every person's day, but I promise you can change one.

As a mom of older kids, I still do things every day that seem wildly insignificant: plunging the toilet after one kid used half a roll to wipe her butt (again), cleaning up unidentified drips and petrified cheese from the rack in the fridge, buying the food, doing a load of laundry and forgetting it until it smells sour and starting all over again. I'm loving my family as I dry-heave while cleaning the bathroom. That matters. Outside my own four walls, it matters to me that I'm loving well and trying to make an impact where I can.

Sometimes when we look at what is wrong with the world, it overwhelms us so much that we freeze. What can we really do for world peace? What can we really do for global poverty? What can we really do to end racism? I think sometimes the answer is right next to us. Sometimes we have to stop thinking so big so we can think small.

My kids go to school in an underprivileged district where the demographic is primarily minority students and their families. I love our school, and I love that my kids are learning alongside kids who have different experiences and speak different languages than them. I am confused by white flight, the phenomenon of white families buying homes in these areas but transferring their kids to schools in wealthier neighborhoods. I have always wanted my kids to have a bigger perspective than our one tiny worldview or the experiences we've had in our home.

I'd bet anything that some of the families who transfer out want to be thoughtful and inclusive—the kind of people who teach their kids to be antiracist. They vote that way; they share memes and articles that way. If they saw an act of blatant racism in front of them, they would step in. But they're missing out on this incredible opportunity that's right at their front doors, literally. They have reasons, most likely. They've heard rumors about the school, or they've seen test scores posted on GreatSchools. But unless you walk in the doors of that school and meet the teachers and the students, you don't know the whole story.

My children have thrived in their school. One of my kids struggled to read and received tutoring from a teacher who became like an aunt to him and effectively changed his life. They've all learned to love pozole and concha. When the 2022 World Cup was under way, Mexico's game against Saudi Arabia was projected in the auditorium and my kids cheered their hearts out with their friends. The whole neighborhood could hear their screams and shouts when Luis Chávez made Mexico's second goal. They've been welcomed into their friends' homes, and we've become family with their families. They've learned new traditions, perfect Spanish enunciation, and what it's like to be the minority, where everyone assumes you're siblings with the only other kid that is your race in school, despite a twenty-four-inch height difference.

I ran into an acquaintance in the produce aisle once, and when they heard where my kids went to school, they looked shocked.

"Oh my," they said, as if I'd told them my kids run barefoot through alleyways at night.

I smiled, hoping to avoid the inevitable conversation. "Good to see you!"

"You know," they said, stopping me, "my dear friend's daughter went there, and it was a terrible experience. She was bullied by another child incessantly. You really need to get your kids out of there as soon as possible."

"Oh, I'm so sorry that happened, who was that?"

"Do you know my friend Mary's daughter, Elizabeth?"

I knew exactly who they were talking about. The child in question is forty-five years old.

I just don't think people realize how little you learn by simply looking at test scores, or taking rumors at face value. Last year, I was picking up my daughter from school when I saw one of her classmates and his parents talking to their teacher. Suddenly, the boy shrieked with joy and covered his face in his hands while tears ran down his face. Both parents and the teacher were hugging and crying. Their teacher told me later that she was giving them the news that he had been reclassified from an English Learner (EL) to Fluent English Proficient (FEP). The hard work that had gone into that process was shown in their tears and joy. Scores don't tell you that.

Last winter I was volunteering at the school to help the kids make tie-dye shirts for their annual color run. I got there a little early and was waiting in the art room for my daughter's class. All along the ceiling were painted stars from different students left over from Christmas. Each one started with *I wish . . .* When I asked later about the project, I was told that the kids each made a wish for someone else.

There were all kinds of things scrawled in handwriting.

I wish my dog could live longer.
I wish everyone in the world had homes.
I wish my dad and mom could visit their family in Guatemala.
I wish my parents had papers to visit my abuela in Mexico so my mom could stop crying.
I wish my family from Mexico could come visit me.

I choked up as I continued to read. I have never had to be separated from my family by borders and legalities. Neither have my kids. But many of our neighbors and my kids' classmates are affected by it daily. It is so very easy for our worlds to become defined by our own experiences and whoever we follow on social media. It's so easy to "know" there is stuff going on and feel compassionate, but also feel absolutely helpless to do anything. The news literally runs off creating fear. It gives us information we need, but the fear and horror of it all keeps us frozen.

I'm no expert, but I think living a purposeful life is simpler than we realize. I can't fix it all, I wish I could, but I can do what is in front of me. I can give my kids the gift of seeing the world through their friends' lives and investing our resources into a school that serves everyone, not just the privileged. It's small in the grand scheme of injustice, but it matters.

Just because someone else has $40 million to donate toward the disaster in Maui doesn't make your $50 less significant. Yeah, maybe mathematically, but being a generous person, doing your part, is what's important. Just because we can't solve world hunger doesn't mean buying someone who is hungry a meal doesn't matter.

I don't know about you, but the times in my life that seemed like $5 moments have always been the ones I will never forget.

Six years after I met the mama in Target, I wrote a blog post that included the story of meeting her and how much it meant to me. The post got quite a bit of attention, particularly from moms who had also been there. I never check my DMs, but for some reason, that day I did. I found this message waiting there:

"Hi Jess, I'm the woman you helped. It was in the Kalispell Target, and my baby was just a week old."

It was her. She told me how much that moment meant to her, and for the first time I got to share directly with her how much it had meant to me. I told her I had left that day feeling like I wasn't alone as a mother. Even though I didn't know her name or anything about her, I knew that if it was me in line at Target the next time, dealing with chaos and barely keeping it together, she would have my back, and that meant a lot to me. It made me realize that I was probably always around a mother or two who got it. I wasn't as alone as I thought. It gave me a sense of camaraderie that I hadn't felt before.

I absolutely love the moments in life that make the world feel very small. We don't need to go big or go home; we actually just need to focus more on what and who is right in front of us.

Impacting the world for good, living out our callings, doesn't need to be an extreme sport. It doesn't need to look like becoming a robot and forevermore doing the right thing all the time. It doesn't need to look like Oprah giving away cars or Taylor Swift giving her tour truck drivers $100,000 bonuses. I love that stuff, but the small stuff matters, too. In fact, I think the small stuff is my favorite.

STEP THIRTEEN: Give What You Can Give. It Matters.

Sometimes I hear about these highly successful people and their routines. They wake up at the same time each day, they eat the same thing for breakfast, they do the same meditation, they do the same workout, they eat the same thing for lunch and dinner. Their day is rigid. They live like a well-oiled machine whose chief purpose is to produce amazing results.

If that's you, I'm impressed, and I think that's awesome.

That's not me.

When I think of living my life like that, I want to cry or scream, or both. You lost me at eating the same thing for breakfast, to be honest, and I was completely gone when you got to lunch. That lifestyle, while productive for some, would be soul crushing for me. I need to eat eggs on Monday and have a fatty cinnamon roll on Tuesday. I need it to be okay if I stay up too late watching Netflix and not even work out in the morning.

Your routine doesn't need to look like anyone else's, and neither does your way of impacting your community.

If there is a global or national issue that really tugs at your heartstrings (but feels overwhelming), try simplifying it and doing something practical in your own community to make a difference.

LIE #14: It's Better to Dream Small Because Then I Won't Be Disappointed

5/11/1994

Dear Diary,

I'm on a road trip and my brother keeps touching me. I made a *clear line* with the seatbelt between us, and he is not staying on his side. He smells like salami and I wish he could ride on the roof.

When I grow up I'm going to have a motor home and I will never go anywhere except in my motor home. There are going to be TVs everywhere and also the walls will be made of pizza and the only person who will have to wear a seatbelt is my brother, even though he will be an adult.

Love,

Jess

I t was the fall of 2017, and we looked like the Beverly Hillbillies pulling up the street to our new rental. It was my first big move in seventeen years. I could imagine our new neighbors peeking through their blinds as the six of us rolled past their Audis in our 2003 Suburban. Our homemade U-Haul was crafted out of a flatbed trailer and spare plywood from Graham's parents' farm. Remnants of spray paint from other projects decorated the sides like a two-year-old's art project. Graham expertly backed it up into our parking place, and all of us (plus our dog, Rex) piled out like we'd recently left one of those religions that doesn't believe in birth control.

I grinned and took it all in. The cool breeze was just as warm and welcoming as I remembered. It had been a long road to Southern California. I couldn't believe we'd actually done it. The jacaranda tree dancing above us was full of purple flowers, and an orange tree leaned over the neighbor's fence, welcoming us back.

"Well?" Graham asked. "Should we look inside?" The kids climbed over one another as he unlocked the door, all of them frantic to claim the boys' room and the girls' room. The floor was dusty, and there was an old-house smell. I pulled open the heavy brown drapes, discolored from years of direct sun. Dust billowed from them like it had in the old cabin on the river. The small yard was peppered with ground squirrel holes, brown patches of grass, and a tiny orange tree all our own. Beyond the fence, the hillside dropped, and the town of Santa Barbara stretched out in front of me with its stucco houses and leafy streets. The mountains glowed as the sun touched them gently. A bell rang in a distant schoolyard. I breathed deeply and smiled.

I reached above me and lifted the heavy curtain rod from its hooks, dropping it and the drapes to the ground. "We won't need those," I said, smiling at Graham.

"What do you think?" he asked.

"I think we did it."

A car pulled up outside and a minute later Aubree's daughter, Gracie, ran through the door shouting for Haven. "It's so great!" said Aubree as she walked in with Roman on her hip and Benji close behind. They ushered in the feeling of home as they hugged us and exclaimed about the view. They'd driven up in their silver Ford Windstar just a few days before to their own rental across town.

The kids raced around, Rex howled, and Benji put beer in the fridge.

My heart swelled as I took it all in. We were living a dream that had started one cold winter evening in our living room in Montana.

When we made the decision to pursue new friendships a decade earlier, Aubree and Benji were some of the first people we connected with. They had been an instant click, people we knew we could do life with. Over the years we'd shared hundreds of meals, if not thousands. I was the first person Aubree told she was pregnant after two years of infertility. She was the first person to visit the hospital after I had my youngest. All of that led to one ordinary yet monumental night sitting on the floor with plates of enchiladas and mugs of wine, talking and dreaming as we often did, but this time was different. We started talking about our town. We all loved it, but none of us felt like it was our forever home. Then someone asked the question that would set everything in motion: "What if we moved somewhere new all together?"

What if . . . I smiled to myself now.

"I'm making pizza," called Aubree from the kitchen. We were home.

I'm a big dreamer. I always know my coffee has kicked in when I start saying sentences that start, "You know what would be cool?" or, "What if we . . ." I dream of trips we could take, parties I could throw, hairstyles to try, tattoos I could get. Dreaming of what could be makes me giddy.

Will all of it happen? No. But could some of it happen? Absolutely. In my experience, every big, outside-the-box, exciting thing starts as a dream. (In case you were wondering, I haven't gotten my pizza motor home yet, which is frankly disappointing, but I persist.)

The real risk isn't thinking up ideas, it's owning them and pursuing them. It's a whole lot easier to leave our hopes tucked into our imagination, like sacred fantasies that provide sanctuary from our day-to-day. Let me check out from this mountain of laundry and toddler screaming on the toilet to come wipe them, and transport myself to a happy place full of possibilities and bottomless piña coladas. Letting those dreams out into the light is a whole lot scarier.

When I was pregnant with Malachi, everyone wanted to know what his name would be. We'd tell them and they would get a look, or they'd say a half-hearted "Oh." My favorite was, "Oh, I knew a guy in high school with that name. Total a-hole." At one point, Malachi's name wasn't going to be Malachi, but the names we had before got so beaten to death by the opinions of literally everyone that we came up with a new one entirely. From then on, we never shared the kids' names until after they were born.

The same applies to dreams and ideas, especially if they're outside the norm. Choose wisely who you share those fragile ideas with, because too much negativity can crush them before they have a chance. I can still remember the look on some people's faces when we told them we'd planned an interstate move with friends. It was a look that said, *Good luck, let me know when you're back.* We had to lean hard into our own intuition and rely on one another for encouragement when we were scared.

It is a mental battle to try something new. If I wasn't aware of my insecurities before, suddenly they were blaring in my face. *Am I crazy? Am I even capable of this?*

There are moments when the fear is tangible, and in those moments we have to cling to the truth.

What if it doesn't look as perfect and wonderful when it's out in the open? It won't. Perfection won't hold up, and every dream has flaws. But that doesn't make it less wonderful. *What if my dream forces me out of my comfort zone? I like being comfortable.* Fair point, and chances are it will. That's a real thing to assess, but in my opinion (and sorry, but I'm right), the risk of living fully alive is always worth it. *What if I can't? What if I get my hopes up and I fail? What if I'm disappointed?* The thing with dreaming is there's always a risk your dreams won't come true. But we're more resilient than we think. We are stronger than we know.

Failure scares me. The idea of trying something and having it blow up in my face is unnerving. Even more, there's the potential for disappointment. What if I succeed, but it's not what I thought? I don't want to wake up my heart, I don't want to let myself be fully alive, only to end up crushed and broken.

We've got to stop being so terrified of failure. It's like the bogeyman for adults. So what if we fail? Everyone fails sometimes. It's not all going to be pancakes and waffles no matter how awesome a dream is.

My kids were (are) my dream, but I promise you right now, I never dreamed of having a house that is covered in muddy dog and Nike prints, sprinkled with protein bar wrappers, and littered with random items of clothing that may or may not belong to one of their friends who slept over. That is the messier part of the dream, the shadow side we don't necessarily envision when we're picturing our future family sitting around the table. You get the table, too, but that table also includes a kid who doesn't know how to last an entire meal without spilling a cup of something, a kid who only wants to eat chocolate and butter, and one chair that for some reason everyone is always arguing is "their spot."

Motherhood isn't what I pictured . . . it's messy and it's hard, but it's also better and it's more. Not despite the hard, but including the hard. My heart is fully alive in mothering. I am doing one of the things I was born to do, and it just feels so right.

Writing a book was another huge dream of mine, and part of that dream involves managing an online community (which I usually love). What I don't love is the horror show that is my DMs. Exhibit A: Randy from Arkansas with a bald eagle for his profile picture asking to chat. Exhibit B: Beth from Florida telling me my cellulite is disgusting and I'm a horrible role model for my kids. Thanks, Beth. You sound like a treat to hang out with.

No, your picture-perfect idea isn't going to turn out exactly like it seemed when it was tucked away safely in your imagination. There are going to be hard parts, exhausting parts, and frustrating parts, both in the pursuing and in the living of it. I wish I could give guarantees. I cannot. All I know is we were meant to live awake.

Side note: What if you're struggling to dream at all?

The other day I looked out my window and saw my teenage son playing with a remote-control car in the driveway. He had a big grin on his face, and for a moment I stopped seeing the seventeen-year-old man-child he is now, and I saw him as a six-year-old boy with big blue eyes and chubby cheeks.

He has a lot on his plate now. Life has gotten more serious. He drives a real car (that takes a lot of gas and money), he has a heavy course load, he is pursuing things for his future, like sports, college, and a career. Sometimes he comes home and I can see the stress in his face. Sometimes I wish I could snatch the weight of it all off his shoulders, but I can't. I do my best to support him with giant sandwiches and smoothies at the end of a long day (teenagers can eat). I listen to what's on his mind and I remind him he isn't alone, but he's in the grind.

Seeing him outside racing his remote-control car up a dirt pile with a huge smile on his face made me so happy. It also reminded me that we can't forget to feed our hearts.

We can't forget to rest and play. Dreams take hard work, life takes hard work, but if we don't allow time to just be silly, we can lose our purpose altogether. If we don't intentionally create time for ourselves, our hearts will fade, and we'll start to forget our why and our what.

If you're too tired to dream, if you're too tired to have any vision for your life, don't forget to play. It can seem like a waste of time if you're focused on all you have to do, but it's not. You're feeding your heart and the little kid inside of you. You need that.

It's an act of bravery and courage to pursue our dreams, and I think it is in the act of pursuing them that our true destiny often unfolds. I know countless people who began pursuing a dream only to realize along the way that their heart was somewhere else. Maybe they started out studying nursing and ended with a degree in marketing. But they would have had neither if they hadn't begun moving toward a dream.

Some of the best advice I ever got was from my sister-in-law Charis. I was wrestling with whether or not I should pursue a trade school I was interested in. I was stuck in a cycle of what-ifs, imagining all the ways it might not work out. If it was going to end in failure or disappointment, I didn't want to do it.

"Ya know," she said, "sometimes you just need to keep walking forward to see if the door actually shuts or not."

❁   ❁   ❁

So, what if your worst fears do come true?

Sometimes you dream something, you work for it tirelessly, you fight through every obstacle that comes up, and in the end, it still dies.

Have you ever been disappointed? (That's a rhetorical question. Of course you have.) Sometimes I think we want adventure, but we want it to be tame, but that's the thing about adventure: It's not tame.

Everyone I know who has courageously pursued their dreams has also suffered great losses. Maybe it's a business they started. They poured all their money and time into it, and it had to close its doors. Maybe it's a marriage that they'd fought so hard for, only to see it end in suffering. Maybe it's the loss of a loved one. Maybe it's a career they loved coming to an end. Maybe it's an athlete sustaining an injury that changes everything.

So why risk it?

A few years ago, a friend of mine and her husband took their first trip without their two young kids. They got their passports in order, and her parents flew into town. She was excited but was also understandably struggling with some anxiety around all the what-ifs. What if her kids got sick while they were gone? What if her parents were overwhelmed the whole time because the kids turned out to be too much for them? What if something happened and they got stuck thousands of miles away? What if? What if? What if? The night before they left, I stopped by to drop off an extra bag they could use as a carry-on, and I snuck a card in the top of her purse.

She texted me on the way to the airport: *Thank you, that's exactly what I needed to hear.*

On the front of the card, I wrote, *What if?* On the inside, I wrote, *It all turns out better than you think?*

They had an incredible time, in case you were wondering.

✿   ✿   ✿

Some of my craziest dreams have come true:

Going on an around-the-world trip with our kids and friends.

Moving across the country with our best friends.

Becoming an author.

Living my *Friday Night Lights* football dreams. (I'm just channeling Tami Taylor over here. No, I'm not the coach's wife or a school counselor, but I am a football mom to a 260-pound offensive tackle, so same.)

Living fully alive is always going to be a risk, but I like the person I am when I choose to do it anyway. I want to live my life. The joyful parts and the painful ones, because they're both a sign of having lived and loved.

It's been six years since we moved with our friends from Montana to Southern California. Every time I tell someone about it, I feel like I'm telling a made-up story. People are confused, surprised, and sometimes intrigued. We move for jobs or family all the time, so why not friendship?

We manifested this dream through fire. We came with the clothes on our backs and the few things we could squeeze into our makeshift trailer. I became an expert in finding deals on Craigslist to furnish our home. My greatest purchase was a mid-century modern Ikea couch and matching chairs for $20. All our beds came from a move-out sale where the sellers were taking nothing with them and everything was free. (Side note, I felt like I'd moved to the land flowing with milk and honey, considering that the thrift store in Montana sold someone's smoke-filled floral couch for $500. Thanks, Kalispell Salvation Army, what a beautiful selection you have.)

Getting our feet under us was harder than we thought. Things were tight financially for a while. We struggled to find jobs that paid enough to support our families. I was boarding dogs and charging electric scooters to make extra cash. Graham was going door-to-door to promote his window-cleaning company and driving for a black car service. Benji was doing Uber at night, and Aubree was selling vintage thrift store finds online.

All our nerves were fried. At one point Aubree and I got in a heated argument about whether or not a red plastic high chair was too big for my garage. She wanted to store it there for when we all had dinner, and I worried it wouldn't fit. I probably could have fit seventy-five of those exact high chairs along with several drum sets, but I wasn't thinking rationally then.

Even when things were tough, though, it felt right.

We'd hustle during the day. Then, a couple of nights a week, their family would come over, or we'd go over there. We'd collapse into each other's couches, open a bottle of wine, and laugh and vent our way through the process. It was amazing to do something that hard and wonderful with people who knew us and loved us so well. It was amazing to be in a brand-new city with friends living close enough that having dinner together required nothing more than ratty sweatpants and whatever was in the freezer. We took turns reminding each other that it was going to be okay and we could do it.

Six years later, we still live one mile apart. The dream has matured past the fragile stage, and we're living it. We continue to love each other's kids like our own. We have matching hoodies for Malachi's football team. One says MOM, one says AUNT. We do not care how ridiculously extra we are.

We have found our groove here. We've become a part of the community, we've made new friendships, and our kids are thriving in all the ways we hoped they would. The best nights are when we combine the contents of our fridges, one of us lights a fire in the firepit beneath our big eucalyptus tree, and the kids bike and scooter on the driveway while we vent and laugh. No one knows us like them, and no one knows them like us.

Sometimes the best dreams won't make a bit of sense to anyone but you, but I think it's one of the best gifts in life that when the world says, "People don't do that," we get to say, "Well, why not?"

STEP FOURTEEN: You Can Do More Than You Think

Do you have any dreams that you're scared to let out into the light of day?

Did you know that anxiety and excitement produce the same feeling in our bodies? Sometimes we just have to flip the script. I went through a period of time when flying freaked me out. When anxiety rose up in my chest, I practiced saying, "I'm so excited about this, I love flying." Believe it or not, it actually helped.

Start acknowledging your dreams. Write them down and share them with a trusted someone. The world is full of open doors if you are brave enough to knock on them. Just because people "don't" doesn't mean you can't. Step outside the box, and practice listening to your heart.

If you're scared, practice reframing. Instead of "What if it goes horribly wrong?" try "What if it turns out better than I think?"

EPILOGUE

Your Turn, in Your Way

When the kids were little, Graham found a long piece of driftwood from an old dock piling at the lake near our house. It's at least eight feet tall, sun-faded into a cool gray color, and worn down so long by the water that if you run your hand down it, it's soft to the touch. It has stood in the corner of our living room ever since. When people ask what I would grab in a fire, that would be it. It's irreplaceable to me, one of my most prized possessions.

I started this book with the story of walking into my mother-in-law's kitchen the very first time. I talked about how it felt to sit around her red table laughing and talking and eating together, and how my understanding of connection and belonging changed in that moment.

Graham doesn't remember a time before that house. He and his five siblings were raised there, along with a dozen others that stayed with them for anywhere from a few nights to a few years. They sold it a few years ago, but when I close my eyes, I can still see it. I can hear the music playing on the radio, I can smell the fresh-baked bread mingling with Marie's favorite Christmas candle. I can hear the crackling of the fire in the kitchen stove and the laughter and chatter.

A friend of theirs stopped by the old farmhouse the other day to talk to the new owner about a truck he was selling. This friend was one of the many non-relatives who'd found belonging in that home. He'd spent countless nights sleeping in their basement and eating meals around the big red table. As he talked with the new owner about the truck, he went silent, barely holding back the tears. Times had changed, but the memories lingered, and the feeling of belonging was forever.

It's crazy the impact a person can have when they stay in their lane, when they do life in their own way, and when they open their home, their hearts, and their table for others to sit at.

One of the features in the kitchen was a doorframe covered in lines and scrawled dates and names. GRAHAM, JUNE 1987. CHARIS, SEPTEMBER 2000. They were the marks of Graham and his five siblings' carefully measured heights through the years. It included other names, too, of people who'd found a home there. It wasn't cohesive or neat. Some of it was done it green marker, some in pen, some in pencil. But it was a beautiful reminder of the years spent running barefoot on the wood floors, eating around the big red table, and growing up together. They carefully removed the wood when they moved.

I didn't grow up in one house. My family moved a lot, and when Graham and I got married and started having babies, we did the same. We've raised our kids in nine different houses, and I know sometimes Graham misses the stability and history that comes with home being the same walls, the same squeaky steps, the same farmhouse sink.

So fifteen years ago, when Malachi was just two, Graham came home from the lake with that massive, worn piece of driftwood. "What's that for?" I asked. He smiled as he propped it up in the corner of the living room, drilled in screws to make it secure, then called Malachi over. He carefully measured his height and carved MALACHI, OCTOBER 2009.

Over the years, dozens of lines have been drawn and carved, a beautiful reminder of chubby hands, tricycles, and a first driver's license. We've moved many times, but that worn driftwood comes with us. It means home, because home for us is wherever we are.

We do home and we do family in a way that pays homage to what we learned from our families, but we've also found ways to make it our own.

Twelve years ago in Montana, our family of (then) five had outgrown the little bistro table someone had given us when we got married. I frequented yard sales until I found a bigger one for $30 that came with chairs. It had forest-green legs and a heavily lacquered top, but Graham sanded it down and refinished it. Paint and pen from the kids' art projects quickly made spots and lines here and there, but I didn't mind. It was a table for doing life at. That was the table we started inviting friends to, so many years ago.

We've created our own space of belonging, our own version of the red table. I tried to make Marie's famous bread recipe a few times, but it never quite turned out. Maybe it was that it never rose enough, or maybe it was some other special magic she put in it. My style turned out to be doctored frozen pizza, things that cook in the Instant Pot (or air fryer), and box brownies. I hope you know that your style can (and should) look like you.

As our friendships grew, our table became fuller. In the dead of winter, Graham's window-cleaning business slowed down, his snowplowing company was constantly in feast or famine (blizzarding or dry), and finances were tight. We'd invite all our friends for a "potato party." We had bacon from Graham's parents' farm and gin they'd given us in a trade. I'd fry up the bacon for bacon crumbles, make gin and tonics, bake tons of potatoes, and everyone would bring toppings and more drinks. Our bank account was low, but our house was full of life, music, laughter, and rowdy card games. We did it in our own way.

I hope you found belonging in these pages. I hope you found rest. I hope you know that you're wanted, that you're enough. I hope you enjoyed the french fries and the five different sauces (I love sauce). I hope you feel inspired to sing at the top of your lungs in your own life (and in your own way), because life is a karaoke bar, not an audition for *The Voice.*

I hope you make your own table, and that you invite others to come and sit awhile. I hope you do it in exactly your way.

I hope you feel empowered to be the kind of woman you've always needed in your life, to champion the women around you, and to create belonging rather than search for it.

I hope new dreams are stirring in your heart and old ones are resurfacing with reignited excitement. Just because people "don't" do it, doesn't mean you can't.

We're all meant to be tall poppies, bright, twisty, colorful, and unapologetic. I like your sparkle, I like your quirks, I like your pizzazz, I like your style.

I'm cheering for you, and I know you're cheering for me, too.

I think if we get quiet and listen, maybe we'll hear all of us cheering for one another.

Women are rad.

Love,
Jess

A LETTER FROM ME

Dear Friend,

Thank you for sitting here with me.

Thanks for listening to my stories, dealing with my favorite 1990s throwback playlist, and letting me stop one billion times to get more snacks.

I hope you know how wonderful and valuable you are. I hope you know that whatever your strengths are, be they kickboxing and business management, or cupcakes and bath taking, you are the perfect one to live your life and live it well.

Go out there and kick some booty.

I'm cheering you on with my whole heart.

Love,

Jess

SOURCES

LIE #1: TODAY I'LL BE PERFECT

7   *71 percent of millennial women*   The State of Women Report 2023, conducted by the Harris Poll on behalf of the Skimm, p. 6.

7   *The top words used*   The Skimm staff, "The State of Women . . . Isn't Working," based on *The State of Women Report 2023*, conducted by the Harris Poll on behalf of the Skimm, p. 2.

LIE #9: ASKING FOR HELP IS A TERRIBLE IDEA, BECAUSE THEN EVERYONE IS GOING TO KNOW I NEED HELP

91   *we don't ask for help*   Andy Lopata, "3 Reasons Why It's So Hard to Ask for Help," *Psychology Today*, June 9, 2022.

LIE #11: IT'S BETTER NOT TO TRY THAN TO MESS UP IN FRONT OF EVERYONE

119   *the number one regret*   A. Pawlowski interview with Tenzin Kiyosaki for *Today*, March 22, 2021. Tenzin Kiyosaki is the author of *The Three Regrets: Inspirational Stories and Practical Advice for Love and Forgiveness at Life's End.*

JESS JOHNSTON lives in Southern California with her husband, Graham, and their four kids—Malachi, Scout, Oaklee, and Haven. She is originally from off-the-grid Northern California and Montana, and she wants you to know that she knows what "real winter" is like (but, yes, she has gotten wimpy and now wears a hoodie when it's 68 degrees, and she is embarrassed about this). She started her career in 2015 with her blog *Wonderoak* (later renamed *Jess Johnston*) when Haven was two years old and life consisted of a lot of diapers and looking for everyone's socks (actually, she's still always looking for socks). She has been featured across national news platforms and was awarded Motherly's writer of the year. In 2018, she and her friend Amy Weatherly created and launched the female friendship blog *Sister, I Am with You*, which quickly gained more than a million followers. They later co-authored two nationally bestselling books, *I'll Be There (But I'll Be Wearing Sweatpants)* and *Here for It (the Good, the Bad, and the Queso)*, and have appeared across many media channels, including *Good Morning America* and the *Tamron Hall* show.

Jess specializes in keeping it real in parenting, life, and friendship. Her jobs include writer, unpaid Uber driver, high school football and middle school soccer super-fan, snack maker, hair brusher, encourager, and mug retriever (from her kids' rooms). She is an avid consumer of coffee and cheeseburgers (usually not together) and is an Enneagram 7 who is always "really into" something new. Her current obsessions are hot yoga, Target tank tops, learning about her ADHD diagnosis, and rings made of sea glass. She will probably not be into any of that by the time she writes her next book.

Facebook.com/jessjohnstonwonderoak
Facebook.com/sisteriamwithyou
Instagram: @jessmariejohnston

ABOUT THE TYPE

This book was set in Caledonia, a typeface designed in 1939 by W. A. Dwiggins (1880–1956) for the Mergenthaler Linotype Company. Its name is the ancient Roman term for Scotland, because the face was intended to have a Scottish-Roman flavor. Caledonia is considered to be a well-proportioned, businesslike face with little contrast between its thick and thin lines.